CARMEN WESTBROOK

Becoming Superwoman

1.0   SEARCHING FOR A CAPE AND BOOTS

Book Design by Nancy Watkins

ISBN: 9781688742505

Website: https://ainagiving.com

CONTENTS

PART 1: RELATIONSHIPS

PART 2: IMAGE

PART 3: VOCATION

PART 4: SPARK

PART 1

RELATIONSHIPS

Chapter 1

WILD RUMPUS

Can I tell you a story?

For decades I knew only one thing about superwoman: that she was this glittering ideal, this weird stepford-wife institutional identity that demanded perfection in practically every perfectly pure picturesque pore. I knew that her power, her strength, her bad-ass knee-high boots came from doing everything *so much better* than everyone else – and oh, I knew that wasn't me. I knew that the superwoman life was literally the last thing on earth that I was interested in or able to become, for I wasn't really all that great, and anyway my heart yearned for freedom, for wildness. That superwoman? She was just kind of... too much for me. And I told myself that I didn't really want that anyway. So while, yes, I dreamed of making my mark and saving the world, I ran away from any kind of greatness, afraid that in trying to become superwoman, I would lose the part of myself that I cherished the most.

I have found that I'm very good at "knowing" things. Yes, well. We'll get to that later, sister-friends. And in the meantime – as every story has to begin at a beginning – we'll start at the beginning of mine.

I invite you to join me here, for this beginning is a gracious place – a place full of wholeness and deep gratitude and maple-tree roots to the center of the Earth. Every time I come here, I close my eyes and conjure the smells – oh, breathe in, inhaling the deep green juniper and the clean newness of damp spring grasses and the slight spiciness of a midwestern early summer field, bejeweled with dandelion crushes and pinkish purple clovers. A sweeping, gently rolling plain of sharply green grasses and the yellow-golden newness of young haymaking that lies somewhere between Nebraska and Iowa, and tugs at my heart with the ache and the longing of youth and simple joy. Gentle winds play with my hair and whisper across my face, for no midwestern plain is ever complete without rough winds sweeping through our identity. In this breezy, cottony, deep-inhaling glory that is conjured in and understood by the most childlike corners of my soul, my toes curl over the sharp crabgrass and forgiving soil and feed my battered adult edges with grace and peace. And when I visit this soul-place, I always end up with arms open wide and spinning around in crazy wild shaker circles, twirling over and over with my face lifted to the rain-sweet smell of the cottony thunderclouds above, embraced by the wide, wide blue and dancing with ecstasy in the season of freedom and laughter. And my toes patter against the grass, rhythmically brushing against the shaft of last-year's harvest and the spikes of the marigolds in the tough hide of my summer-worn soles.

Have you ever gone out and danced in the torrent of a midwestern spring storm? And I don't mean the dark, green-yellow brooding of the vehement Nebraskan thunderstorm. I mean the drenching, playful, toe-squelching spring rain that jumps on you suddenly as you're curled up on the couch, calling out to you to come play, play, play in the flowers and with the earthworms and under the sheltering arms of the shivering birch leaves. And you run out of your door laughing and shaking a bit at the silliness of it – for what will the neighbors think? – and the moment you lift your face to the cool speckles you forget to care and start spinning for joy and song and ridiculousness. And the bright-gold marigolds at your toes seem to laugh and invite you to be a part of their silky petals and remember that fairies, in fact, do exist.

Such is the life of a girl raised in Nebraska. And, oh, it would be so beautiful to end there, wouldn't it? To leave it all to simplicity and fun and rain-soaked adventures?

Ah, but of course – every thunderstorm comes with its own type of lightning. And no midwestern town survives without its specific brand of dark underbelly. And so there are always also the cold, stultifying rivers of inky blackness that are interspersed along the route of the wild things in the dancing rumpus of our souls.

At the end of this twirling soul-dance I always collapse, exhausted, and climb onto the flat glacial rock that must inhabit my dreams from our summers in Minnesota – for the gray stone, sparkling with graphite and mica and containing all of me, has no place in the chalky sandstone beds of the deep Nebraskan undersoil. And as we clamber onto the stone and collapse on our backs, the rock's immense there-ness gathers under our shoulders, and we feel the incredible gratitude that pours out when you find something totally immovable, that has been there long before you and will continue on, regardless, long after you're gone.

Do you know what is my favorite part about that rock? It's the feeling of pressing my palms flat flat flat against its rough, slightly gritty gray surface. And the feeling of warmth that soaks into me from this hard, immovable protuberance – the feed-back from the rock's tryst with the sun, soaking into our shoulder blades, the lower back, the backs of our knees. And the spreading of our fingers wide wide open, strangely cool to the touch under our palms – isn't that odd how that happens? And, oh, the smells and the sounds! Deep puffs of clover and fir-wood and damp maroon soil unbroken by the deep deep silence of peace and rustling pine needles and intermittent birdsong.

And the second-best part of the rock is when we quiet our breaths, melting into the peace and stillness around us, and open up our breastplates to slowly, slowly start feeling the tilting of the Earth. The tilting and – yes just a bit of spinning – that you can be a part of, play a hand in creating, when you meld your body to the Earth and *listen*. Listen to the sounds of the earth talking to you – for, in the farm country, the Earth speaks truth – and joining in the rhythm of the hidden stars as they spin in their cosmic dance.

All of this, in one little midwestern plain.

This is by far my favorite place to go. It is the place of security that I found in my childhood. I suspect that we all have such a

place – that place of quiet and peace and soul-smoothing. And...
I'm happy to share mine with you whenever it's needed. Lie be-
side me on the rock, if you like, and feel the security and the
grip of the Earth as we all go tumbling through this cosmos together. Look up to the immense, unending blue blue blue of the
sky, and maybe even explore a bit of its wideness.

And slowly, into our vision creeps a lone prop plane, small
and scattered in the wide expanse of the light blue spinning
sky. This wee plane is so small that it seems a part of the peace,
and is an unending font of curiosity as it buzzes quietly in the
sky, passing overhead and across our screen of vision. How on
earth did it get there? And what is such a small, indomitable
plane doing in the great expanse? Can it really be a part of this
silent earth-ness from before the dawn of time? And it is almost
a lazy curiosity, because our hearts and our souls are so en-
twined with the never-ending cosmos dance – what can such a
tiny speck really do in such eternity? And how can it ever contain itself?

For myself, I pause in my quiet tilting and smile sweetly at
the plane, my heart thumping a bit louder and inhaling big, deep
breaths of satisfaction. Because, you see, that plane contains my
mother – and in these moments I see, for the first time, a woman
escaping her confines and letting her dreams soar.

After the divorce, my mother decided she needed to do
something to support herself – and, I suspect, something to escape the confines and the gossip and the breath-crushing corset
of the small Iowa town in which we lived at the time. So, like
Amelia Earhart, she became the literal pilot of her own life,
charting a course through all of the dimensions, and leaving

behind all of the heartache and the trouble and the stories that she just "wasn't good enough" to do it all.

Recently a very dear, very inspirational friend of mine said "I'm tired of everyone saying 'I've had a tough child-hood' or 'I've gone through terrible things' as a justification for their ability to fight for justice, tolerance, and those that can't do it alone. You *don't* have to have experienced terrible things in order to help others. We can all pitch in, because we all know pain."

I invite you to hold that in your heart as we walk through these stories. Because it is as true as the day is long – we all feel the same depth of pain. And we all feel the same leap of joy, if we allow ourselves. If I have learned one thing in life, it's that what-ever is the hardest thing that you are going through it is *the hard-est thing for you*. There is no yardstick on pain. Pain is pain – we feel it equally. The pain that you are going through right now, the biggest struggles that tear at your soul – for we all have them, sister-friends – are no more, and no less, painful than any other's. Nobody gets the monopoly on heartache – or joy. And there is never, ever, an uncomplicated story.

I grew up in an incredibly loving family. My mother, brother, and sister are perhaps the most amazing people I have ever known. My parents divorced when I was two, and from there my mother, an incredible woman, raised us children to be loving, strong, and wise. Herself from a troubled family, she walked through that childhood fire, then the subsequent fires of heartbreak, divorce, and poverty, to come out on the other side an incredible mum. She told us that, early on in her parenting journey, she sat down and had a talk with the

Universe (she called that force God, and please feel free to call it Vishnu or Ra or Odin or Plant if that works better for you) and determined that all of her strength would go into being the best mum she could be. And man, she succeeded, didn't she? Come what may, she put all of her being into raising her kiddos. She taught us all the lessons we needed to know – glittering sapphire waterfalls of love and rugged gray granite mountains of discipline – and poured every particle of her being into each one of us children, uniting us as a tribe that has been the bedrock and foundation of every step I've taken in this world. I am truly, truly blessed.

And at the same time, the first ten years of my life I grew up poor poor poor – I mean dirt poor, cockroach-rentals and ramen lunches cooked for us by the more affluent neighbors and tear-stained cheeks as my mother drove away from the daycare at 5am poor. And I was forced by the divorce decree to visit an abusive father every other month, visits that were filled with fear fear fear, sadness and loneliness, and binge eating to stuff aside everything that happened there. I had sex for the first time at 15 to my also-lost drug-crazy boyfriend, struggled with bouts of bulimia for part of a decade, and felt that there was no place in this world that was meant for me.

No story is uncomplicated.

This is a story about superwomen. This is also a story about loss and weakness.

This is a story about fierce women standing together in a sisterhood of determination. It is also a story of betrayal of those fierce women, and the overwhelming messes that life creates.

This is a story about women changing the world. It is also a story of apathy and disbelief. It is a messy story, as all true stories are. It is complicated, beautiful, destructive, and restructive. It is a journey both of the smallest individual and of the biggest forces that are blowing across the globe. This journey begins with one heart, one soul, one spark, and ends with a conflagration that is engulfing us all. It is, of course, a journey that begins with one story.

That story is yours. And it's mine. In the end, actually, I think we can call it ours.

Shall we dive in and begin together?

Chapter 2

THE CRASHES THAT MAKE US WHOLE

I think that one of the things we should talk about at this point is my intense belief that we were made to be in relationships with each other. In fact, I think that perhaps that's a cornerstone, a lodestone, in the building that we build and name "the point of life." For me, in my life, I know that I've found each piece of the puzzle that is me by seeing it reflected in another person – and oh, it's amazing and terrifying to be that mirror for others as well. And...I get ahead of myself.

Did you know that babies left in orphanages without human touch wither and die? They can be completely bodily taken care of – fed, changed, kept warm in blankets – and yet, without that human touch, that human connection with another, they will "fail to thrive" – the medical terminology for a baby that, for no physical reason, slowly dies.

Oh, so it has been for me in my life.

I loved the 2004 movie "Crash", not especially for the scenes or the cinematography, but for the immense underlying theme and the quote that underscores it – "You brush past people, people bump into you. In L.A., nobody touches you. We're always behind this metal and glass. I think we miss that touch so much, that we crash into each other, just so we can feel something." Crash into each other. So often that is exactly the way it has been for me as well.

I have a friend – an incredibly wonderful, loving man – who witnessed his father murdering his mother when he was just a wee boy. Crash. He is, amazingly, one of the kindest, most hilarious, most thoughtful men I know. My mother was raised in an incredibly abusive household – her mother having been abused by *her* father. Crash. And my mother was somehow, through that, able to pull it together and become an incredible parent, doing the full 180 turn that would change the future of all of the generations to come. During my childhood, I was intermittently subject to abuse of my body and soul by my biological father, just like 1 in every 4 people on Earth. Crash crash crash. I have friends that were raised in incredibly loving families, surrounded only by warmth and care and nurture, that routinely crash against the people around them as they discuss and unpack and repack their values, their beliefs, what it means for them to be human and for that other person in front of them to be human. Oh, the crashing comes in every life, doesn't it? It's a matter of when, not if.

In his amazing classic, *The Road Less Traveled*, M. Scott Peck says (and I'm paraphrasing): It's not a surprise that some of us are messed up. What is a miracle is that we're not all complete nutcakes.

Crash. Crash.

We all crash into each other, over and over, don't we? Like electrons in a charged environment, we crash parts of ourself up against parts of others, transferring energy and feelings and memories, one to another, as we wildly dance our way through life.

There's been some amazing research done lately on memory, work that has fundamentally altered the way that I think and move with the people in my life. Basically the new memory story goes something like this: we now understand that we store some of our memories in the people around us – thus freeing up our brain space for more processing, and for storing *their* memories in us. For me, in practice, that looks something like this: "Hubster, why was there a war in Syria, again? And – I can't remember – what does it have to do with us?" and my husband replies with the information, which I then weave into whatever story I'm telling at that cocktail hour. And he, similarly, stores the names of every one of our relatives, children's teachers, children's friends, and occasionally the names and ages of our children (all very important and pertinent information in our lives) in my brain, as those happen to be the memories that I'm the best at. It's lovely and wonderful, actually, to have someone else there with whom I can store those memories – it creates this invisible web between us, binding us together and holding all of our puzzle pieces together so that we don't go flying apart like so many atoms in a supernova. It's the same, I think, with pieces of our selves.

As memories – at least for me – serve as markers of "who we are," this storing of these pieces of our memories in others also serves the dual purpose of storing the pieces of ourselves. And then, of course, it's the duty of those that love us to remind us of those pieces when we forget. "Yes you can do this – don't you remember how courageous you are? Let me help to remind you...and surely you can do this, too." And those memories we store in others, those pieces of our selves that our friends, our colleagues, our lovers, our families hold for us – they are all of the pieces that make up us. And that means that each of us is, in fact, a part of the whole world. And that something precious is lost, is shifted, in the web whenever we lose one of those pieces, one of those people that stores that information for us. And of course, there's another side to this as well. Because those stories we store in others? Sometimes those stories need to change. And ohhh, hello crash.

For me, there have come many moments throughout my life when I've had to decide how much of my future was going to be determined by my past – my past memories, my past stories. And while my past will always be mine, and always play a part in how I think and approach the world, my future actions are mine alone – they are not slaves to the past. In fact, I've found that it's been my duty to claim my destiny instead of allowing my past to claim me. And so, in those moments when I've been able to look at my past – truly and openly, look at it and not reject it or abhor it or judge it, just look at it with acceptance – and decide that that chapter is closed and another needs to be written, those moments have usually been accompanied by a crash. Or...well, often, lots of crashes.

Do you have those moments when someone says something to you that irks you unreasonably, and that statement or question or observations or whatever sticks in your soul and irritates your insides, like a burr stuck in the paw that just won't come out? I've found that those are often precursors to the crash, the opening salvo in a part of me that needs to be changed, needs to be rewritten. For whatever reason, those anger-moments are, for me, one of the ways the Universe chuckles in my direction, points its finger at me, and says "time to do something about this."

And each of those finger-pointings come in the form of a crash with another human being.

And so, just like an orphaned child, I've come to claim this intense belief that we desperately need our relationships with each other in order to *be* – that these relationships not only hold the kernel of who we have always been, but also the kernel of who we are to become. In fact, it's become such a strong belief of mine that I've pursued it as one of the pillars of my superwoman life – like the pillars of Edoras, it holds up the foundation of everything to come. It's just my job to hang on and enjoy the ride – and trust that the others are there for a reason, even if literally none of it makes sense at the time, and I wished it were another way.

Chapter 3

RELATIONSHIPS 1.0
ALL OF THE HIDDEN VOICES

The first thing you might need to know about my early relationships is that I don't remember them very well. Everything before the age of 10 is very spotty and quite vague. I think this was a blessing given to me, as it seems that these years were too rough and tumble for my budding self to understand. And yet what I do remember are the gifts these roots gave to my life.

When I was ten, my mother got married to my stepfather (a lovely man – not untroubled himself, but who isn't?) and took us to relative safety from our poverty-stricken beginnings. Before ten the memories that I have are just snapshots of life – laughing, laughing, singing, and yes, occasionally fighting with my brother and sister in the safe cocoon of my mother's home, interspersed with going to visit my father and flashes of darkness and suffocating and fear fear fear. And, because no story is uncomplicated, I also have images from my father's house of playing dress-up with makeup and clothes with my step sisters, diving into the depths of the summer swimming pool together, eating melted Twix bars and drinking coke. And underlying it all is the terror and the darkness of knowing that he would come after me again.

For me, I like to think of our life stories like giant willow trees, with each of us as the silvery dryad inside. With their deep deep roots to soak up the goodness and the pain, and their tall, wide branches to dance in the wind, sway together, and reach the sun, we are all anchored to the relationships of our childhood as we blossom and move. The story of every life begins with the roots – and while my roots are complex and tangled deep underground (oh, and aren't they all?), they are also shared with people that I love with all my heart. And this, of course, gives me great strength – as do all roots that are tangled and trapped together.

In my years of working and living with people all over the world, I have seen and felt the realness and truth of a well-known leadership "ism." The -ism is that of our Sparkle-ism: namely, each one of us has an amazing, incredible, phenomenal diamond of a soul. Truly. Every. Single. One. Of. Us. I have shared in seeing how awesome, how lovely all of our different sparkles, our constellations of rainbows are – and how much each sparkle makes up the diamond that is inside of each one of us. I marvel at the beauty of it all, and thank God for this incredible creation, because, man, each one of us is so unique, so different – and so *incredible*. We all have this rad, amazing soul inside of us that's been hugged and shaped and faceted by the world. It is so very awesome. And it's so very, very covered in the poop that life shovels on top.

My sister often says that childhood was so confusing for her. And while I don't feel exactly that way, I know what she means. For me, childhood is that time of discovering what that diamond actually is, and getting help with uncovering it while at the same time getting more poop shoveled on.

My mother, while not perfect, definitely helped me with taking off some of the poop. Being a former prop plane pilot and full of flight herself, she realized at some point that my personal diamond was desperately in need of wings. And so she read my soul and got me a She-Ra costume. And if you don't know who She-Ra is, it is time for you to put down this book and go find a YouTube video. I'm not kidding. I'll wait. It is absolutely worth it. Because She-Ra is the princess of power – and dangit, every little girl needs more of that in her life.

And you know what? That outfit was *rad*. Wielding a cape and shiny fabric boots and a sword, I was indomitable. And indomitable is what I needed to be. Clearly my mum read my soul a-right, because, while I don't have many memories of that time, I do remember that freaking fantastic She-Ra costume. In it I was invincible – I was the Princess of Power – I was the woman my secret soul was whispering to me. My mother and my brother and my sister were my rocks – and provided the counterbalance for my relationship with my biological father, which was decidedly a poop-shoveling-on kind of a relationship.

I'm not exactly sure what that means. I have memories of...blurred terror. To this day, when I try to remember my time with him, I feel like I'm being physically slapped in the face – I flinch away as if something is hitting my face. I like to think that those slaps are my brain, still trying to protect me and lock away all of the secrets into memories that aren't yet safe. I'm not sure. And what I am sure of is that there was a time when my father, the one that was meant to protect and cherish and teach me about all of my wonderfulness, used my essential nature, the part of myself that I loved and treasured the most, as a tool against me. And I remember the terrors of him taking a possession over me that was so total it encompassed and intimidated and frightened every part of my soul. And I know that for so long, for so long, all I wanted to do was to please him and have him – or, God, just anyone – keep me safe. And I know he took that sense of security away from me, and instead turned it into a story of shame shame shame and guilt that it was all my fault for being me.

I remember particularly the day when my father learned that my mother was getting remarried. He stood in the doorway of the bedroom and told me that, just because she was remarrying didn't mean that I was safe. To quote the memory, he said that "I could never escape him" – and my stepmother coming up from behind to shush him from doing more.

And do you know something? He was right. I never could escape him – and I will never be able to. Why? Because parts of my soul are defined by parts of the souls of everyone that has been in my life. And I think, maybe, that's true for all of us. It is in relation to others that I have been given the gift of finding myself amidst the tumult and uncertainty of life. And while that terrifies me in relation to him, it also gives me incredible freedom. Because, you see, while I can't decide how other people treat me, and I can't make all of my relationships turn out safe and loving and ok, I *do* get to decide exactly how I get to act and who I get to be in my relationships with others. And I do get to decide what's important to me, and what's not – and make my life based on that.

I think that's the real gift of all of these early relationships that we all get to be a part of.

And so while yes, a part of my childhood story is one of fear and terror, a part of my story is also one of intense love. And I guess, in the end, the point isn't what exactly happened or didn't happen in those relationships. It's not about how great of a mother or father I had, or how many friends I gathered in high school. It's about finding out who I was in those relationships. And I think that our earliest relationships give us that gift. They give us this intense time of folding ourselves into the parts that work, of rubbing up against and finding the rough edges of the parts that don't work, of finding out all of the facets of our own diamonds so we can turn them to the light and let them sparkle the most.

And wouldn't it be amazeballs if we could all sparkle at our highest wattage?

I have an image in my mind that anchors me to that feeling of a rad little woman – an image of me standing on my front yard, in front of the one tree on our postage stamp of green outside of our teeny tiny red barn of a duplex, wholly shiny and holding my sword up high. It is, in fact, the story that I choose to dwell on about my childhood and what defines my soul. It is the story of strength, and fun, and freedom, and womanness. Because, fellow Superwomen, the stories we tell ourselves shape our destinies. And that story gives me the wings to fly.

I invite you to fly with me.

Chapter 4

LIFE-FIRES

In my experience life, occasionally, sets in our path a fire to walk through. And each of us is given the choice – to walk through the fire, or to skirt it to the side. If we choose to skirt it, that's fine – absolutely fine. And if we do, a little while later life will hand us another fire – only this time it will be larger, being at least the size of a bonfire. This is not because life is vindictive. It's just because it's the *rules*. And if we then do decide to walk through that fire instead of skirting it, and if we do so while also holding true to ourselves – we will get through on the other side. And, oh, on the other side there is always a rainbow. There is, waiting for each of us, an incredibly magical, amazing gift. That gift is different for each person and each fire – and it is exactly the gift that we will need in that moment.

I was once asked by a sister-friend if I really, actually believed that. And here was what I said to her: "I don't know if this is a fact. I can only say that, in my life, I have observed it as a law, like gravity. We don't KNOW if gravity is a fact, because we cannot positively prove it. And we can say that it is a law – that, 100% of the time, so far, it's worked – the apples fall down, not up. Same story for life-fires. You avoid them, they get bigger. You walk through them with love and faith, there's always a gift at the end.

Chapter 5

RELATIONSHIPS 2.0 – MARRIAGE

We have a problem with intimacy and truth in our society right now.

You know those marriages that you look at and see the couple still holding hands, seemingly completely in tune with each other and creating some kind of underground music together that you can feel and only they can hear? And then you turn and view your own slovenly, slightly lazy, itching-himself, hairy husband and think to yourself "why can't I have something like that?"

What if you already have it and you just never knew?

My husband and I got married when we were 22. *Twenty-two*, y'all. Babies we were. And, honestly, we both knew it – we both felt way too young to be married, and we both also knew that if we didn't marry then, we most likely never would – and that was too big of a risk to not take.

We met in college at a party orchestrated completely by my sister, when we were both 19. My sister had been pestering me for months to meet this cute guy that she thought I should date, which was awkward to the extreme as I was pretty seriously dating a guy from another university and spending 150% of my income on going to see him in Nashville every few months. Finally, apparently out of desperation, my sister threw a party just to make us meet. And meet we did. He was this cute guy in a baseball hat that had this totally kissable sweet contained smile – and I was *completely* uninterested because I was in another relationship.

Funny thing, that – apparently the universe agreed with my sister because, when my to-be husband called me two weeks later to ask me on a date, I was newly single off the heels of a "we've been dragging this out long enough" breakup.

In traditional teeny-bop pop culture movie romances, this is where the movie would end – on the fantastic first date that promised the perfect future.

This isn't a teeny-bopper pop romance.

My to-be husband, this young wonderful man of 19, summoned the courage and the strength to call me and ask me out. Can you imagine what I did?

Yep. I didn't remember him.

Like, not at all, people. Not one bit. And while you might think that being rejected is the hardest answer, being unmemorable might be far worse.

And as my husband stuttered through "I'm Jon? Jon Westbrook? The guy in ROTC? We met at your sister's party, I'm in her Freshman Interest Group?" My adult been-together-for-two-decades self is keenly aware that this would just be the first time that I would hurt him. That this embarrassment in front of his friends (because, of course, he called while his friends were in his room), this sticking a sword in his soul emblazoned with the words "you just might not be good enough," was just the first in a long line of fire-brands.

It was, of course, a sword unconsciously wielded – as many of the early ones in relationships are. And is it just me, or is it one that grows double-edged in the shadows of every marriage? A sword that is wielded by all of the dragons inside of us – and turned with ferocity on the ones we love the most? And oh, sweet soul, that terribly and often means ourselves, too.

And now I get ahead of my story.

Mercifully, this Jon-that-would-be-my-King took me out on that first date, despite my unrelenting forgetfulness. And we started dancing the heart-tearing soul-song of deep love together. That's actually a metaphor, by the way. We've only been able to actually dance fantastically together once in our lives, and I'm still trying to figure out how to duplicate the experience.

We withstood breakups and the death of friends and the trials of distance and separation to finally come to an evening in my newly-married sister and brother-in-law's L.A. apartment. My sister (bolstered by many a rum and coke) looked my to-be husband in the eye, slapped her left hand on the table, and said "you need to get my sister a ring at least as big as this one if you're going to marry her."

Crash.

Let me explain something. A) Jon and I had never discussed marriage up to that point, B) my sister has a *really* nice ring, and C) we were 21 at the time, had zero money, and Jon was going into the extremely non-lucrative career of 2nd Lieutenant (the lowest ranking officer) in the Army. Oh, sisters. They are the best, aren't they? It's always good to have someone that has your back, even when you don't have your own – and aren't in the same boat with them on whether you need a diamond in your ring.

Poor Jon – he left the apartment and walked around the block to un freak-out, only to come back to find my fantastic bro-in-law in a staged fall from his chair to take the pressure off. I am not kidding you. I told you, these people are the best. And while we all look back on that night and laugh at our ridiculousness, I also believe that maybe, perhaps, this was another twist of the sword, the beginnings of a seed of doubt planted in Jon's heart – the fear of a wonderful, thoughtful, caring 20-year-old that was now taking on a huge weight of responsibility in the form of a family.

Well, the universe works in odd ways. Because the next morning we woke up to my brother-in-law knocking on our door and saying "guys, come out. Something's happened to the Twin Towers."

Yes, I'm not kidding. Next morning. Hello, universe.

And all through that day of uncertainty and worry and doubt and questions questions questions, there was one anxiety that underrode it all –

What did this mean for *us*?

Well, since this marriage was taking place in the heart of GWOT, my hubster (to his credit) told me that 70% of these military marriages end in divorce, and that the statistics were against us. And that he'd be gone all the time. And what I heard was that I had to give up my career and follow him wherever he deemed. He told me, in short, that we were doomed.

What he didn't know quite yet was that I was a pigheaded mule, and take any bets against me as a personal challenge to my abilities.

I decided then and there that I would beat the odds (and yes, you read that correctly. Enter the forehead slap. I had no idea what this marriage thing was all about). I decided that, come hell or high water we weren't going to be a part of that 70%.

God, I had no idea how hard that would be.

Our honeymoon was a wild ride through the wilderness of America to the nest of the Deep South. And yes. It was totally a wild ride. And oh, the fantastic memories from that trip – seeing the wildness of America, reading Lonesome Dove to each other as we drove, eating as many corn nuts and Dr Peppers as would fit into my as-yet unadorned wedding dress. One of my all-time favorite memories was when we were pulled over in a citizen's arrest because our trailing Pathfinder was swinging wildly back and forth, obliterating the lane markers in the high winds of Montana.

It was fantastic. And oh, I love that free, fun, wild couple that we were and are so very much.

That dispersion set the tone for our marriage to come – driving as carefree, slightly desperado-ish style gypsies through the unknown wilderness, not necessarily equipped for the journey we'd undertaken, and sometimes slightly out of control, creating collateral damage behind us. And also singing, telling stories, and *being* with an intensity that both creates and destroys everything within, too.

Our honeymoon, in fact, was like a microcosm of the years to come. We, over and over, set out into the great unknown, completely unprepared for the adventures that await us, and we continue to do so with laughter and love and, above all, togetherness. And while that has come with its costs, damaged each of us intensely, and caused a *lot* of pain occasionally, we've come to realize that no great masterpiece can be created without destruction before. We lived, on that trip, through our very first mini-fire; and that set us up for the bonfires to come.

That first year of marriage was a life-fire for sure, as anyone that's been married can attest to. I had to walk over the coals of growth, falling down again and again. The only difference here was that I had my partner's hand to hold onto while doing so. The coals don't burn quite so much when they're shared.

Oh, it was wonderful, too, don't get me wrong. We made love like rabbits, anywhere and everywhere across our tiny apartment. And we also fought with nails and hammers and occasionally nuclear weapons, sometimes making scars so deep as to come out years later. That first year of marriage is *hard*.

Georgia, our first duty station, held the sweetest little apartment in it that I decorated with whimsy and broken futon couches and lots and lots of love. It was our sweet love nest, and it grew the first year of our tiny beginnings in love.

We fought about *everything*. Toothpaste (he was in favor of it, I was in favor of not being in debt). Drinking (he was in favor of it, I was in favor of...not being in debt). Money (he was in favor of spending it, I was in favor of...not being in debt. There's a pattern here). Extended family (ohhhhh, and that's a whole other book right there).

I remember one epic battle in particular when we were on a vacation with my family. Having absolutely no money to go on this vacation, and feeling compelled to do so to maintain the family unity, I had pinched pennies (i.e. no toothpaste) to scrape up the funds for what we felt was our obligation – we both value family almost above all else, and have a terrible tendency to sacrifice all that is us to make the family happy. We were finally on the vacation and having, in fact, a bit of a honeymoon together. It was really, really wonderful and fun – enjoying rum and coke and the beach and just time together. And then we started feeling the pressure to spend more money than we really had. I remember one night in particular when all of the younger generation (my brother and sister and their partners) wanted to go to a casino – and my hubs wanted to tag along. I hope all of you money-managers are currently in a state of righteous indignation with me, because I still haven't gotten over this. A casino?? A CASINO??? When we couldn't afford toothpaste??

I finally relented and said he could have $20 to spend and have fun with. And I have still not heard the end of that story on my miserly ways. Yep, Superwomen too feel the slings and arrows of the world.

And that was pretty much how we managed to set up our relationship and marriage that first year – me being the responsible parent, him being the rebellious youth. Me leaning in 200%, him standing there with his hands at his sides while I fell down over and over. It *sucked*, let me tell you. And it wasn't what I had envisioned. And at the same time, I'm pretty sure it's what got us through those first 8 years when he was constantly deploying and I was constantly doing everything else.

And while having children and more deployments and moves every two years would serve to break us more and more as we were clinging together for dear life, do you know what was the one thing I wanted from him in all of that agony? All I wanted – all I ever wanted – was for him to turn to me and say "how was it for you when I was gone? How is it for you on the inside? What are you feeling right now? I can only imagine the pain and hardship you go through each day, just living this thing we call Life. How is it for you? I hear you. I hear you. I hear you, my love. And oh, my heart is with yours in this agony you've lived alone. I see you, my beautiful heart. I see all of the pain and agony you've been through, and I see this brilliant diamond that has continued shining through it all. I see you. I see the hurts and slings of the world that has beaten your beautiful heart. And oh, I could not love you more. Come, let me stand by your side and wrap my arms about you and tell you how much I love and adore this partner that I get to walk through life with. Thank you. Thank you, sweetheart, for loving and living and sharing it all with me. Thank you, my soul-shine."

I imagine he wanted nothing more than exactly the same.

We have this thing right now with intimacy in our society. When my husband and I went through the real troubles – the troubles that finally drove us to marriage counseling and therapy and him picking up a relationship book on his own volition (you know it's bad when…) – he came to me one day with this revelation that there is a difference between intimacy and sex. With sex we can feel that possible vulnerability, that physical opening up to each other that can lead to a temporary release on the valve of aloneness. And with true intimacy – the sharing of our *selves*, our authentic inner being, in all of our vulnerability and faults and beauty and weakness – we find this incredible hurricane of possibility and acceptance and togetherness and love love love that awes us all into tears of gratitude and strength.

And right now, in our society, we're leaning *really* heavily on that sex crutch.

And do you know what? I don't blame us. Not one freaking bit. Because sex is easy, people. It's super freakingly easy. It's fun. It takes a bit of that pressure off. It makes everything feel a little bit better.

It's the 50 shades of gray that makes the darkness more bearable.

Unfortunately for us there are only 50 shades until we run out of gray. And then we're just left to face the darkness alone.

My husband and I found this out the hard way. And before you let your mind wander and go down a track that's untrue and not helpful to anyone, no we aren't those 50 shades of gray. We have a healthy sex life and we love to be with each other. And we found out that, in the end, none of the fake intimacy could ever be enough.

And then our marriage fell apart.

I remember after our first son was born, I threatened to move out. I was completely justified – he had gone out at my brother's wedding and gotten so wasted he passed out, puked all over me and the baby, and passed out again for me to clean up the baby and the antique bedspread at our immaculate pre-wedding B&B – and I was convinced this was the worst our marriage would ever face.

Sister-friend. I was wrong.

When we'd been married for twelve years – *twelve years*, people – I found out that for seven of those years, our relationship had been built on sand. Yep. You did that math right. Over half of our relationship we'd been insanely falling apart.

And in the next 6-9 months it *all* came out – all of his pain from the deployments, all of his pent-up anguish at turning off all of his emotions for decades in order to survive, all of his lingering poop from a messed-up childhood (who *hasn't* had that, btw?). And I had to sit there and take it.

Can I tell you something? I don't admire women that stay with crappy husbands. Not one of them. Hillary, you should have thrown that clown over years ago. You are way better than that. And can I tell you something else? When the time came for me to decide what to do about this never-right situation – I realized I was just like them.

And I realized that if, somehow, by the mercy of God, we could walk through this fire together, the gift on the other side would be that thing that I'd been searching for all my life.

It wasn't easy, people. Good Lord. That is the understatement of the century. It ripped my insides out and set them on fire. It strangled me and writhed in my stomach and made me weep torrents of daggers. It made me both hate myself and wonder in awe at the strength that had somehow filled me as he would hit me with words of "I never really loved you" and then fall in my arms sobbing at how hard it had all been.

I mean. Screw you. And at the same time, so much love for this poor, broken diamond.

Of course, it was two broken diamonds that wept together.

I remember that, during that time, we would go out on dates and work *so hard* at rebuilding our us. And after one of those dates, a friend from the neighborhood said to me wistfully "I saw you and your husband holding hands walking to the bar the other night. You guys are so awesome. I can't remember the last time my husband and I held hands." And I just remained quiet and smiled mysteriously at her, because I was so afraid they might all find out. I learned later, so much to my sadness and shame and guilt at being too weak to speak the truth, that she and her husband divorced.

We have a problem with intimacy in our society.

Because what I found through all of those tears and all of that therapy and all of that living and walking through the fires – what I found was that, in the end, what we really both needed the most was to allow ourselves to be broken. And to lean *into* each other in the brokenness. And to allow that to be ok. And to tell other people about it too, say the words out loud, so that we could all share the strength in saying "me too."

To be broken and unsure of what we were going to do next. To be broken and so scared that we might not be good enough, strong enough, attractive enough. To be broken and lost and angry and alone alone alone as we walk through this sometime-fire that is life. To be broken and admit our dragonishness and wrongdoing and stupidity and cowardice. To be broken and to hold open our chest and show the defeat and say "this – this! This is what you married! You thought I was amazing! You thought I was pulled together! It was all a mask I put on to get you to marry me, to love me – and now you see me for what I TRULY am, and you have the full permission to ridicule it to death."

To be broken and vulnerable, oh so vulnerable, to the point of hideous agony, and hear in return "I hear you, oh beloved. I see you, my heart. And it is what I have always loved about you the most. Because, in fact, all of these scars from all of that brokenness are just different facets of you and only make you sparkle all the brighter."

We have a problem with intimacy in our society.

And it makes sense, doesn't it? It makes sense in our age when it's so easy to divorce, when we can always just move away if we don't like the area, where we can unfollow people and friends that don't say the things we like. It makes so much sense, right? I mean, who wants to bare their soul when we look around and think and believe that the most likely outcome is that people will say "ewwww" and turn away?

Crazy thing is – usually baring of the soul leads to exactly the opposite.

It took a lot of convincing of my husband that it wasn't going to end that way for us. And he wasn't physically abusive or put me or the kiddos in harm's way, so we had that safe space in which to find each other – anyone that doesn't have that I recommend you get the heck out of dodge. And I swear it was that 70% divorce rate gauntlet that he'd thrown down on 9/11 that kept us together. I am basically too pigheaded and stubborn to be that statistic. Really. I hate to say it, but I think the secret to a lasting, loving marriage is being too persistent to let it go.

So I want you to turn and look at that slightly smelly, kind of lazy, hairy pile of personhood that's next to you. Or I want you to look at that next possibility in your life, the one that you met the other day and thought "good Lord NO, I couldn't have that amazing marriage that I want with *that* person." And I challenge you to ask yourself:

"What if that marriage doesn't look like the way I thought of it before? What if, in fact, it was so much less – and so much more?"

And can I tell you something else? I sit on the couch nightly and look at my slightly smelly, slightly lazy, *very* hairy husband and now – *now*, after years of pain and soul-bearing and continued not-knowing-what-the-hell-we're-doing-now I say thank GOD he's nothing less and nothing more than this smelly man that has, in fear and trembling, agreed to share his firewalk with me. Thank God.

And one more thing, superwomen. Throughout our whole marriage, our *whole* marriage – to include the good, the bad, and the very, very ugly years – we have been told that we have something special. That there is something about us. That there's some kind of soul song that we play together, that only we can hear and everyone can feel.

And while I now smile and say thank you, we both – you and I – know the truth behind the hand-holding. The truth of a life lived together that's been messy and mistake-filled and wrong. And the also-truth of a story of devotion and courage and love love love. And do you know what I always tell them?

Don't believe the lies – and it's a helluva lot harder than it looks. And do you know what? The music is MAGIC.

Looking back on those first few years, I realized we'd made one very crucial omission:

We'd gotten really, really good at uncovering the dragons inside. And we'd gotten really, really good at pointing those dragons out to each other, and saying "spend some time with those dragons, because they are engulfing you." And we'd forgotten to say "And you know what, my love? I love you precisely because of those dragons. They are the dragons that complement my own."

Big mistake. Huge. And it just made the fire that much bigger. Because the only thing that douses the flames of life-fires? Massive, overwhelming waterfalls of love. And those waterfalls grow much larger when there's someone else contributing to the inundation.

Chapter 6

JACOB'S LADDER

I used to think that the point of conversation was to convince others of the validity of my point of view. Over the years, I've changed this belief to now see conversations as a way to connect with another human being and, perhaps, discover something new about them and myself. It is the difference between debating and storytelling, or work and play. In work, we are there to make something that fits the image that we have in our minds, whereas in play we are there to uncover and unleash unseen potentialities.

I'm still kind of a basher. Don't know if you've noticed? My apologies. Apparently my old habits (and Germanic roots – Germans can sometimes be bashy, too -and I can say that because... Germanic roots) die hard.

When I was young – about 11, I think , on the cusp of entering junior high – my brilliant older brother put together a speech for our high school's forensic team. He would practice it occasionally in the evenings in front of my family in preparation for a big upcoming tournament. I have images of me sitting cross-legged on the floor, warmed by the fire in our large brick fireplace, with the orange light playing over my brother's face, illuminating it with warmth and mystery.

I sat enraptured – my image of myself is with huge eyes, glued to my brother's face – listening to the story that he wove, my world slowly widening. My brother's speech was about the vagaries of humanity in High School – and this was the uncharted, mostly terrifying land into which I was about to be thrust without a backward glance. And even more than that, his speech was a story – and not *just* a story, it was a performance, a transfiguration, a transmigration where High School became the jungles of South America and each teenage group became a different form of animal.

It was brilliant. And, man, as the cheetah-jocks roamed with the monkey-nerds, it gave me hope, if only in the glimpse of understanding.

I don't know about you, but I consistently find that life is hard. Like. *Hard*. Fist bumps to Buddha on *that* fundamental truth (first rule of Buddhism: life is suffering. Second rule: get over it). It's hard. Really, really freaking hard. Which doesn't mean that I give up and climb into despair (occasionally there is a climb beneath the blankets, yes…). What it does mean is that I work hard to make sense of it, to understand what the heck it all means, and why things happen the way they happen.

My brother's story helped me put a frame around my upcoming junior and high school existence. His words helped to give me some understanding of what it would all mean, and how I might find my place in it all. And while it was hard to understand, and so hard to live out – oh, how incredibly boring the existence would be without that struggle.

I mean, seriously. Snooooooooooze.

Can you imagine what life would be like if we were all born exactly the same, knowing all of the answers (that, of course, would be the same), with everything figured out? I personally used to think that would be paradise – no more strife! No more struggle! Just endless bliss!

Do you know what I think about it now?

BO-RING.

Because, while my brother's story was full of hardness and pain as all of the animals of the high school jungle interacted with each other, it was also full of hilarity and movement and action and *life*. Can you imagine what the conversation between the cheetah jocks and the nerd monkeys would be in the perfect-world scenario?

"Hey."

"Hey."

And, um ...that would be all. Like, zero more. Zero. They couldn't talk about how nice the day was, because they wouldn't know the opposite of nice. It would just be...the day *is*. They might not even be able to say that, because without strife there would be no death, so...they wouldn't even know what the meaning of *is*, is.

So, yeah. They'd be stuck with "Hey." And while, occasionally, that is the actual sum total of conversations between adolescent boys, we'd like to think it's a bit more for the rest of us.

For the rest of us – the cheetah marathoners and the monkey silicon-valley kings, the conversation is much more like this:

Monkeys: "Why do you keep *running* so much on the ground? *Way* easier and more efficient to be swinging in the trees."

Cheetahs: "Dude, have you ever *run*?? It's like all of your muscles come alive at once, and you're sucking into you all of the fecund world around us with every breath. It's like the definition of freedom and me-ness and universe-ness all at once. Also it gives you great legs. Highly recommend. Why on earth do you sit up there in the clouds, instead of feeling the Earth beneath your feet?"

Monkey: "Hello, muscle-brain, have you ever seen the world from up here? It's like you can understand the *whole point* while floating effortlessly above all of the ridiculousness and minutiae and, you know, bugs down below. It lets you see how everything is connected and how all of the webs and networks work together. It makes me feel tiny and huge all at the same time ...Huh, I never knew that that was why I loved it so much until I just said it to you."

Pause.

Cheetah: "Well, that's pretty rad. Guess I wish I could see that sometime."

Monkey: "If you come and sit with me, I'll tell you more about it. But only if you let me ride on your back during one of your marathons...think I'd like to feel that."

"Deal." "Deal."

Well, poop man, that's a hell of a lot more interesting than just saying Hey.

Recently I was on a plane to Nairobi and was seated next to an amazing woman. Flying to help set up some more nonprofit work in Kenya, we started talking each other's ears off about leadership development – something we are both passionately devoted to. And, given that it's a 10-hour flight, we ended up becoming fast friends and spoke about things that are only allowed to be spoken about between lifelong friends... or the odd transition-land of strangers on planes.

We talked about religion.

So I am a converted Catholic (more on that later). I have friends (and family) of literally every different religion and non-religion possible. I rank very, very high on the open-mindedness scale. And I love talking to people about it. It just happens to be a pretty off-limits topic. So when I find someone that stops in their sprint down below, and pauses in their swinging from the trees, and meets me halfway to just chat and learn from each other...oh, man, I am *all in*.

And so...we talked. And we explored. And it was *fun*. And in speaking with her, I said something that I hadn't known I believed before. I said "I think we have all of these different religions and beliefs in the world so that we can struggle with other people about it, think about it, feel about it, learn more about ourselves and what that even means, learn more new doors that can open up before us, tread new wild pathways that were already waiting in our thoughts to be discovered." (I said it much less eloquently than that. And that was what I meant).

And you know what? After I said that, I thought "Whoa. Didn't know I even *thought* that."

Recently I read about the Anlo-Ewe culture, a group of people that have a much bigger definition of our senses than the standard Western definition. And one of the senses that they have defined captured my soul and gave it wings – because it is exactly how I've felt about it, I just didn't know how to express it. One of their senses is the sense of *talking* – and how rad is that??? Basically talking, speaking, is a sense, because it helps us sense what is on the inside of us. It helps us sort through all of the 900 words that are washing around in our brain every minute, and it helps us choose the most important ones to express in the only 150 words per minute that most of us can actually speak. Because the beginning of every spoken sentence is an adventure – we are never quite sure exactly where it's going to take us, how that sentence is going to end. At least for me, in my self...I start off a sentence having a vague idea of what I'm trying to express, and often the end of the sentence helps to define that idea even more. Or sometimes, the end of the sentence isn't quite right, and I can feel the slight disconnect. And in the best of times when that happens, I have someone with me that is willing to go exploring with me, willing to duke it out or jump off cliffs of thought with me or maybe disagree completely with what I'm saying and stay in the conversation to see what happens. And then maybe the struggle with each other really turns into a game, a hilarious ball of muddy children rolling and laughing together as they forget that the adult point is to win and instead play the game where the winners are the ones that go on the wildest adventure.

In the Bible, there's a story of a man named Jacob who wrestles with God all night – and is named Israel, literally the father of the 12 tribes, for his willingness to go all in and wrestle his way through. And he's given as well a dream of heaven, of the ladder that leads up to paradise. I kind of don't think it's a coincidence that the one that's willing to wrestle it out is the one that finds the ladder.

Mudballs and childsplay and ladders and paradise. Way, way more fun than just plain "hey," IMHO.

Chapter 7

RELATIONSHIPS 3.0 –
THE FRIENDS THAT SAVE US FROM
THE CLIFFS OF INSANITY

Once upon a time in Neverland there lived a fairy gypsy rebel, who fought great lonesome battles against the dirt-smeared local trolls. Covered in feathers and bedecked with scarves, our fearless fairy waged the warfare and the battle alone, protecting her homeland from the ravages of disbelief, dishonor, and trembling insincerity. She often played games with the trolls, besting them in feats of catch-a-mouse, peanut-butter charades, and blueberry dodgeball. The trolls especially liked the games that involved food.

One day, in an especially gruesome battle of stuff-the-biscuit, our flighty fairy caught sight of a particularly hairy troll – and his muscle-oaf fun caught hold of her heart. Alone and rebellious, she wrapped her scarlet scarf around his neck and claimed him as her own.

And as the years went on, our fairy rebel forgot her rebellious ways and covered her gossamer wings with raiment of respectability and adulthood. And while she was ever-so-small, she was also ever-so-determined to win this battle, too.

She was also ever-so-alone.

And so as she bowed and scraped and lost her play, our colorful fairy realized that one was not enough. She realized that rebellions are only won by the determined and the numerous. So, she set out to gather an army.

One by one, the rebellion grew, and our fairy queen dusted off her gossamer wings. As she flitted through the Neverland – building a nest here, stopping for a sip there, dancing and singing and stomping through exotic Eastern countries, creating and breaking and strengthening in the Americas, and finally twirling and falling and flying into the Old World and the dawn of time, she found her partners in the rebellion dance, the ones that would sing and laugh and love with her. And she stored a piece of her glittery-ness with each one, and they with her, so that each became refracted jewels of each other's rainbow souls, reminding each other of who they are – and what they were there to fight for.

Our fairy queen fought many battles, some with chocolate and catapults on the outside, some with monsters and dragons on the inside. And through each battle her rebellious fairy sisters stood by her side, catching her in their brilliant scarves when she fell, swaying their hips and laughing at life to remind her of who they were in each other.

And together they climbed the ladders of paradise.

My friends have saved me from the cliffs of insanity. And the more I grow, the more I realize just how much I couldn't do any of this without them.

I used to think that the strongest and most successful were those that could do it alone. I thought that to really by Superwoman, I had to prove my mettle flying solo. And the more and more success I see in my life, the more I realize how wrong I was. Oh, how wrong wrong wrong.

The Superwomen that we've known in the past – the Amelia Earharts and the Marie Curies and the Eleanor Roosevelts and the Helen Kellers – they all, all of them, every single one, had a secret weapon:

They had friends.

Like, the dead body kind of friends – the friends that, when you show up at their door in the middle of the night with a dead body, get out their shovel and help you bury it, no questions asked. The friends that hate your enemies more than you do, so you can find space in your heart to forgive, knowing that you're still safe. The kind of friends that go to Chilis with you every week with your two under-two kids, even though they have no children, because you just can't take it anymore and Chilis has the best air conditioning. The kind of friends that come over for coffee or weekly dinners because your husbands are never home and *you just need to adult sometime*. The friends that love you through your craziness and your betrayals and your terrible childhood shame and let you cry cry cry as you drive and sing along to everything Bette Midler. The kind of friends that hold your hand and call you on your poop and remind you of what you're fighting for.

The kind of friends that never let go.

And so, while our fairy princess assembled her army to lead a rebellion and save Neverland, she realized that, while doing so, her fairy rebels had, in fact, done so much more.

They had held onto each other's diamonds and treasured them more than paradise itself.

And oh, the dance has been so beautiful.

And that, my beautiful sister-friends, is why relationships matter. Because in relationships – true, intimate, we're-all-leaning-in and loving relationships – everyone holds hands and refuses to let go. And when each of us has that safety, that security, we, each of us, can let go of our fears and take flight to discover our own rainbow-diamond. It's a pretty rad dance, let me tell you. And I can't wait to keep dancing it with you.

THOUGHT QUESTIONS

Chapters 1 – 3

1. What are your thoughts about "Superwoman?" If Superwoman does do it all so much better, how does that feel to you - inviting, exciting, despairing…? Do you have a wildness that calls to you, or is it something else?

2. Do you have a "childhood place" - someplace safe that you go? Can you imagine it? What does it look like? Smell like? Taste like?

3. And the inky blackness in the wild rumpus - where do you find that winding its way? If you had a "hardest thing" in your life, what would it be? And what is that "hardest thing" that you are confronting in your life right now?

4. What about this section makes you the most angry? What rattles you? Why?

Chapters 4 – 7

1. Who are the 3-5 relationships that hold many of your memories and pieces of your self? If they were a circle, who would be in the next circle out? And...the next circle from that?

2. What is your story of a perfect committed relationship? Is it of marriage? Is it forever? Is it holding hands while the car swings wildly behind you? Write out the top 5 points of what that looks like for you. How does that contrast or compliment where you are now? Try to see your person in that new light - where might you be standing together in this?

3. If you could say one thing, just one, that you have been saving in your soul and have been wanting to share, what would it be? (don't worry, you don't have to share this answer! This is just for you to ponder).

4. Who are the friends that have saved you from the cliffs of insanity? What is the commonality in those friendships? What do you discuss the most, do the most, how do you act with each other the most? Jot down a few thoughts here. Who are you in those relationships? Are you the savior, or the one being saved?

PART 2

IMAGE

Chapter 8

LIONS & LIONESSES

Some time ago, when I was very young and much wiser than I am now, a lion came to my doorstep.

He was large, and warm, and furry, and bold. I rubbed my fingers through his mane and knelt in awe of the power that emanated from his soul, even as he sat.

He nudged my soul and whispered in my ear "you belong to me, now, little one. For I am your beckoning, and you are my guiding light. I call you forth, oh singing lioness."

His great golden light surrounded and enveloped me, and I felt a great, great longing – for what I did not know, and it pulled my heart to tears and determination.

It took me half a lifetime to find that siren song that he had put inside of me. I lost my path and forgot how to dance as a lioness. I buried myself from the love and laughter that waited for me there, and traded it in for duty and diminution. It has not been an easy prowl, nor one I would have put upon myself. But it has been MY prowl, and oh – it's been beautiful beyond my lonely imaginations. Thank you, oh my captain, for giving it to me in such great faith. I have now realized that you, my heart song, have been dancing the song of the light all along.

I am honored beyond belief to prowl with you. Let us sing this song together.

Chapter 9

IMAGE, 1.0

I started throwing up when I was 16 or 17 years old – not quite sure, as my memories of those years are slightly faded, possibly due to the pot-smoking and late nights with my overage boyfriend. I can't remember much about the bulimia, except that I felt that I needed to get it *out*, I needed to abandon this feeling of self-loathing and disgust and make space for the love love love that also resided in me.

We are such complicated beings, aren't we? We, delightfully, have so many different sides – to quote *Anne of Green Gables* (one of my favorite books), "there's such a lot of different Annes in me...If I was just the one Anne it would be ever so much more comfortable, but then it wouldn't be half so interesting."

I've not always been grateful for all of the different parts of me. When I was younger and in hiding, all I could think of was that if anyone saw me for who I really was, they would hurt me again – in whatever form. And so I put on a lot of layers of paint over my diamond. And for me, that meant paint in the form of extra weight. I would put on that extra paint, covering myself up, because I just couldn't stand that they would all see me for who I truly was. And then, blessedly, if I was covered up in all of this extra weight I could have an excuse in my soul for not going out and being with people, because I was ashamed of how I looked and had no confidence and so I could just say "I'm not going out or trying to make friends tonight because they'll just reject me because of my weight and I just can't deal with that."

I think, maybe, that there are other people out there like me. I do know that a goodly amount of this came, for me, from being sexually abused when I was younger. And I know that one in four people experience that in the world (even if they can't remember it – most of us don't remember it until we're in our 40s). And so…I think it's possible that many people, for many different reasons, use their image as an excuse to hide themselves from the rejection and hurts of the world.

That was most definitely my story for quite some time. And, occasionally, it's a story I still reopen and try on again and again and again – as is true for all of my deepest struggles.

Image is such a complicated topic, especially for women, isn't it? At least that's true in my circles – it's somewhat taboo to discuss it, like we'd all break under that topic like so many pieces of flaxen straw. As if, in discussing our images, we're touching on something that lies too deep inside, too buried, and we all just need to accept it at face value that "this is what I look like so just back off and let me be." Funny, that. We can all talk about so many things – our professions, our favorite drinks, our families and number of children, even politics and religion before that – because that's the one thing that's off the table. It's more acceptable to ask why your friend voted for that political party, but ask them why they decided to dress like a preppy mom instead of a frump? That's off-limits. In fact, I'm pretty sure the word *frump* is just downright illegal.

Vicious cycle, that putting on weight to hide myself and then using it as an excuse to not go out or expose myself to the world. And it worked. It worked for a long time – it kept me in a cocoon of safety. And then one day...one day the butterfly that was inside had had enough. To this day I still don't know why. Perhaps it's just because I'm an inherently impatient person and was tired of waiting to live. And so that butterfly took out her jackhammer and started going at it from the inside of the cocoon. And she said, quite loud and clear, "*No more*" – and forced me to go out into the world. And from that moment on, I realized that my image was also a part of me. That it was an outward reflection of what was going on inside my soul. Just like when you enter a person's house and it's decorated in Georgia O'Keefe and flamboyant reds and oranges. Houses reflect who we are, just like the house for our soul (our body) reflects and dances with the essence of us.

Oh, wouldn't it be so *fun* if we could all talk about this? Terrifying, yes. And also so, so fun. Like, butterflies with jackhammers fun.

Chapter 10

JUDGEMENT

Warning: This chapter contains some gnarly language. Apologies in advance. And it was the only way I could figure out how to say it.

I don't know if I'm alone here, and I am often haunted by the story that I am a failure if I don't do it all, I must live my life a certain way to be a success, and that if I want to be an accepted part of a group I have to do (fill in the blank here).

To which I have recently started saying "FUCK THAT." And oh ...it's soooooo good.

I lived for far too long feeling the constant judgements – or the assumed judgements – of the society around me. I felt, almost constantly, like I wasn't living up, like I wasn't actually doing enough, and that, in fact, I pretty much needed to never eat, work out constantly, eschew sleep (and cheese), love everyone better, and frankly just try harder. And if I did that I might, just maybe, not be a failure in the eyes of everyone.

Maybe. And I don't know if I'm the only one here, and I do know that I've lived under that brick for Far. Too. Long.

Brick. Ha! That doesn't even come close to describing it. Universe-smoldering, mind-drenching, fusioning me into an ever smaller and smaller atom until I become pure energy anger crushing agony begins to come close to the feeling. For me, it's like the fist that grips with claw-like fingers around my heart, digging in as it squeezes every feeling out of me until I'm a robot of perfection.

And it's complete, total, and utter crap. And yes. That's easy to say. And to feel?? Oh, man, I still struggle with that.

I've studied Superwomen throughout the ages because, frankly, that's what I heard people telling me I needed to do. And when faced with a problem, I do what all true children of chemistry professors do and I study it. And I kept trying to fig-ure out *how they did all of the things*. How did they get it all done and keep their sanity? What were their secrets? And while I did learn a lot of secrets along the way, one of the biggest secrets that helped to click it all into place was this:

Superwomen don't do it all. They just do it differently.

Did they work harder, live more gorgeously, be more perfect than everyone else? Nope. You know what they did? They became unfuckable at a really young age.

Let me explain.

Have you ever seen that skit "Her last fuckable day"? Hilarious. Awesome. Seriously, Google it. It's about a late 20s-something starlet in Hollywood, surrounded by her older starlet sisters, being told that she's no longer going to be cast in the fuckable roles because she's "too old." She'll now be cast as the stepmom, the next door neighbor, the divorcee. Because she's now over the hill. And they're toasting to her last fuckable day.

Oh, to be unfuckable.

Do you know what happened when I started getting older? I stopped caring about what other people said about me. I stopped caring about their judgements, their opinions and I just started doing it my own way.

Superwomen do that. They just do it younger than the rest of us.

Yep. That's it. It's like you put an unfuckable 45-year-old into the body of a 28-year-old. All of the worry about others disappears, and suddenly that woman shoots off into the stratosphere and *starts flying* because she's living life on her terms. That's it. Become unfuckable. And then you can start reaching those stars that are calling to you.

So what does that really mean? Because, like I said. Easy to say. Not so easy to do. Well, there are two steps that helped me, personally, along the way:

Step 1: Figure out what matters to you. Figure out what your values are. When you're 80 years old and fistbumping your girlfriends to a life well-lived, what do you want those fist bumps to be about? Family? Career? Great tits? I'm serious, who cares what other people say about it? All that matters is what matters to you. For me, freedom and independence rank almost exactly equally with family and friends. Which makes life complicated, let me tell you. And you know what? Everyone else can go jump out a window if they think I spend too much time on my own, or too much time with my family. Because everyone's got an opinion on that. And I don't really care – because I'm the one that's going to have to be looking back at myself in the mirror when I'm 80. No one else. So. My only job is to figure out what matters to ME.

And Step 2: Soooo...this is a big one. And this is one that I still have to talk with myself about. Basically...I've found that, if I want to stop caring about the judgements of others, I have to, myself, stop judging them.

Oy. Vey.

Ohmygosh can I tell you *how freaking hard that is*?? Because I am a problem-solver. Also, I'm a member of society. I constantly find myself saying "if only they did it this way, they could *fix* that thing!" or "whoa, she should do this to fix that." I mean. Look at this book. Look at what I'm literally writing right now. I'm saying that if you want a better life, stop judging others. Which, in itself, is a judgement. Yeah. It's a thing with me.

AND...I've found it's the only way I can muddle my way through without caring. Because while I can tell you my story, in the end, this is just my story. This is just what's helped me. I have literally not one clue if it will help you. I'm *super* curious to hear if it does. And I'm also super curious to hear what other things have helped you. And I don't have all the answers. And holy bacon I still need the help. And frankly I think that people (and, really, mostly women. Sorry menfolk) are really, really rad. And I love to hear their stories. And that curiosity, that storytelling – that has been one of the best things that's popped me out of judgement. Because I'm not the one with all the answers. I'm just one of the women, muddling through this amazing life together with other women, and trying to love and do the best that I can do.

So my current rule on this is: Don't give a rat's ass about how anyone else does it. Love them. Include them. Marvel at how incredibly different they are from you. And then let that hot potato drop. Don't let it turn into judgement. Because, in the end, you quest your way – and I'll quest mine. It's a total bitch to do, by the way. I think this must be why monks live on mountaintops alone – because it's so *hard* to be all zenned out down here in the poop. And yet...it's the only way I've figured out how to be unfuckable. And unfuckable is one of the things every Superwoman I've researched stands for.

So here's to you, fellow kick-ass Superwomen. I wonder what it would be like if we instituted a ban on judging each other? Like if stay-at-home moms, working moms, non moms, older women, teenage girls, transgenders, lesbians, pro-lifers and pro-choicers, atheists and bible-thumpers – what if we all just kind of hung out in the poop together? I kind of wonder if that's what's been secretly keeping all of us down – that the judgements that I learned to impose on other women when I was really young were exactly the things that kept us all back from showing our superpowers. From taking flight. From fixing the world. And you know what? I have no idea. I just think it would be really, really rad to try it out.

Chapter 11

IMAGE 2.0 – ANTM

"We delight in the beauty of the butterfly, but rarely admit the changes it has gone through to achieve that beauty."

Maya Angelou

That quote is, and always has been, the chapters in the story of my image. Just when I get to the point when the dance feels perfected, when I feel like the image that projects *me* to the world is just right, something fundamental shifts and I have to rename it all over again. And let me tell you something – it is *freaking frustrating*. And I also try to convince myself that I wouldn't have it any other way – because how boring would it be to always be the same?

I learned a few years ago that a woman typically sticks with the same makeup and hair look for roughly seven years. I think that timing is so interesting – and significant – in light of the theory that we all go through seven-year cycles in our lives, one block being growth and introspection and attempted understanding, the next block being going out into the world and bashing it over its head to form it into the image of our current understanding. So we are constantly swaying, every seven years, between the being of trying to understand, and the doing of bringing that out into the world and effecting the impact that is being called in us to do.

That pretty well coincides with both my internal and image life, looking back. Kind of wish I'd known this when I was younger, perhaps I wouldn't have been so angsty. Or, well, I probably would have been. I've never been known for my patience.

I personally find it really, really hard to let go of that "what was" self – even if I didn't love it – because at least it was *known.* So while being a smoking bulimic wasn't necessarily an image that I loved or wanted to actually live out, it was something that I understood, and it was therefore pretty comforting. Stepping off into that abyss – the abyss of *not* smoking, of *not* throwing up, the abyss of being a mom and an adult woman? Freaking terrifying. I didn't even know what that meant – except that I'm pretty sure that it meant something frumpy and with prints.

Enter Holly.

Holly and I met while I was stupidly pregnant and she had a brand new baby. Sweltering in the heat of a North Carolina military barbeque (and sweltering in the way that only super pregnant or nursing moms ever can), I remember that she struck me with her peace and laughter in this momlife, even in the midst of a massive diaper blowout during the most inappropriate moment. I, on the other hand, stood in my sweat-rolling angst-ness, internally roiling with the mom life that had been surprisingly thrust into my lap and all of the ankle-swelling gigantic-thighing discomfort that came with.

So yeah. I invited her over for brunch. Because that's what you do as a military spouse. You brunch. And coffee. And clearly I needed this woman to brunch and coffee with me.

Now Holly is a Christian Scientist. Which means she's largely been pooped on her whole life for her beliefs. And I grew up right next to a Christian Science church, raised by Chemistry professors. Which meant that not only did I actually know what a Christian Scientist actually believes (helloo, not scientology), I also didn't give a crap what she believed in or didn't believe in. And that meant that I got all of the awesome-ness, all of the friendship, all of the Holly-ness that Holly had stored up in her fab self – all of the fantastic diamond that is Holly and no one ever saw, I got that all to myself.

That first brunch was right after the birth of our kiddo numero uno. We were knee-deep in renovations of our house (yes, that timing was an interesting decision on our part…), and Holly came in and just *looked* at the bare studs and the nails sticking out all over the place and made no bones about how crazy she thought we were. And how much we could do it if we wanted to. She just thought we were crazy. And then I served her my South Beach frittata (trying to lose that baby weight…). And she totally let me know that she thought it was disgusting. Not that I was disgusting for serving it, or that anyone was disgusting for liking it. Just that she thought it was disgusting. And she laughed the whole time she was saying it.

I knew then that I had found a diamond in the rough.

How many friends will actually *tell* you what they feel??? And how many of them will tell it to you, without trying to change you??? In my experience very, very few. And so Holly climbed into my heart from the very get-go. And she's left a number of beautiful gifts behind for me to discover on her wanderings.

The next few years – before the cruel, cruel military world separated us from living in the same state together – found us mostly inseparable, attempting to figure out this whole mothering thing and motherhood image together. And one of the biggest things Holly gave me was – and is – a non judgemental love of style. She showed me – not through words, just through life – that our image is this glorious reflection of and dance with the soul that we are on the inside, and that, while nothing can touch our eternal souls, our image can help us express them and reach out and touch and connect with others. And by image I don't mean just our bodies, because our bodies are us too. I mean the aura, the presence, the us-ness that we put out into the world, reaching out in silence for us to all of the world around us, saying "here I am! Let's play together." It's the way we move, the clothes we wear, the way we arrange and design and decorate our houses and spaces, the style of our makeup and hair and the way in which we enter a room.

And she taught me that with ANTM.

Ok, soooooo...who loves Tyra Banks? Anyone? Anyone? Smize??? Seriously. I can't get enough of the smize.

ANTM stands for *America's Next Top Model* (and if you didn't already know that you're dead to me). For years it was our dirty little secret (so...not really on that dead to me thing. I hid it away because it was just *not* ok for me to love it so). We stayed up late nightly, binge watching episodes while our husbands were deployed and our babies were snoozing, snuggling into our separate chairs and eating black bean brownies in the darkness as we laughed and critiqued and discussed very seriously everything from clothes to poses to crazy ridiculous photo shoots to the contestants that were kicked off. We both took it seriously and laughed our asses off at the results and at ourselves for loving it so. It was glorious.

And somewhere in there, somewhere between Holly's professed love of paisley and my crazy v-neck sweaters, a little boat came chugging through the waves and into my soul and meandered through the byways to disperse the message that *I was ok*. That my image, my old image, my new image – there was a healing. And that just because Holly loved paisley and I hated it didn't mean that one of us was right and the other was wrong – it just meant that Holly looks good in paisley and it expresses her self in the way she wants to show it to the world, and that man, it just *doesn't* for me. These nights and laughter and style and love gave this girl that had hated everything about her body and her image and her self that was reflected therein, this girl that had repeatedly beaten up her body with throwing up and cigarettes and terrible food – those nights gave that girl a bit of dance healing. A bit of fun. A bit of Tyra Banks smizing and love from a friend and the absorption that it doesn't have to be all drudgery and hardship. That we are here to dance and have fun and express ourselves joyfully in this being that is oh such a part of us. And that all of it is to be revered and joyfully lived out – because, dangit, style is *fun*. Makeup? Totally fun. Braiding hair together? Yep. Fun. Working out and doing yoga and feeling amazing all day, every day for it? Freaking Phenomenal. Taking the time to make delicious, super healthy food? Frankly, that's a dancing sport. And shoes and boots and really any accessory are just *amazing*. End of story.

What I found in the paisley mist is that there is nothing to deride or judge or feel guilty about in any of that. There's no part of me that gets to feel guilty about leaving my kiddos or husband to work out. Heck. No. Because it's *fun*. And joyful. And because, at least for me, this is how I let the world know my inner self, how I reveal myself to them, this is how I show myself in color and movement and light and pencil skirts – and oh, it's an amazing self. It's joyful to let it whirl out there in purple abandon.

Do you know another thing that I learned during that time? I learned that no one, *no one*, gets to make me feel bad about my body or my self. No one. Zero. No one gets that power over me. If I look at a model on TV and start feeling bad about my body, that is *not* her fault. Or the producer's fault. Or the media's fault. Heck. No. That is *my* fault. My fault for not honoring myself more, for not prioritizing myself, for not making the time to care for and protect and nourish and love myself, inside and out. No one gets to make me hate my body or try to hide my being. Because when I am doing all of those things, I couldn't give a rat's ass if I don't look like those models on TV. I've had three kids – my garden of stretch marks will attest to the fact that I will never look like them. And do you know what? When I look at those women, I think like Holly. I think "huh, she can totally be that way. She can rock out that paisley. And I can look my way and rock out my v-neck shirts. Because that's how I love my body." And I will never, never, never turn my daughter to an image of a model and tell her that it's the model's fault that she feels bad about her body. Because I refuse to be a body-victim my whole life, hating my body and letting that hate take away my power – because *nobody* has the power to make me hate my image – that is 100% up to me and what I do about myself. And that is the lesson I will always teach my daughter – she is never a victim in this world, and so if there is something she hates, it is her *duty* to do something about it. And if she hates her body, it is her *duty* to take care of it, to take the time and the energy to do something about it – not blame that hate on someone else.

And so, instead of teaching my daughter or myself or my friends to feel powerless, I will, instead, take the time to figure out myself and teach my daughter how to love and nourish and protect and care for our bodies, so that she will never, ever, ever hate herself. Because I've tried it both ways. And one way leads to puke and self-loathing, while the other leads to love and laughter. I choose the love and laughter.

And, I think that maybe that will be the way it is for my whole life. A constant shuffle of learning and relearning, of

breaking the old and letting it go, of loving what I was and figuring out what I am now – and just as I have that figured out,
accepting that it will change and morph into something new
and fantastic.

Chapter 12

STORYTELLING

Every morning I wake up and place the silver chain around my neck. I pause and take a moment to feel the comforting weight of it, the cold silver pressing against my skin and settling into that little scoop just above my breasts. The cross forms a protective barrier here, a shield between my vulnerability and the hurts of the world. Like the fairytale bible that stopped the bullet on the way to piercing the heart, my cross is my daily protection – my breastplate of armor – that creates sanctity for my sometimes battered soul. And oh, how I guard it jealously.

Ok, so remember how I am a converted Catholic? For me, that means that I was raised (vaguely) Protestant, and then when I was in my 30s converted to Catholicism. I've discovered that, at least for me, life is full of many paradoxes, and the joy is in holding all of them within myself, sifting and sorting through them like colorful sand running through my fingers. It's beautiful to be the archeologist of my own soul

– and dancing with others in the multi-facets that sparkle within the discoveries of their selves.

My inner world has always been peopled – or, occasionally, animalled – with a colorful cacophony of seeming disparities. And they would, in their wild abundance, have overwhelmed me – if it were not for the one overwhelming voice of the Universe. For me, that voice has always been the voice of a Lion, and it has been a voice that has given me immeasurable comfort throughout it all. And that availability, that strength of the always-voice from my Lion Captain has been, truly, the greatest gift of my life.

Many years ago, while I was at University, I read a book that explored the interconnectedness of the Universe. In it, the scientists were discovering the flow of energy between plants and humans – and back again. There were beautiful (and frankly pretty weird) descriptions of how our thoughts can actually influence the people – and the plants – around us. And how we all are connected by this massive amount of energy.

I'm telling you – weird. And it wasn't weird because I thought it was untrue. It was weird because it was voicing out loud all of these thoughts and feelings that had called to me from my core from my very earliest memories, and that I had pushed and smooshed aside – despite their slime-like ability to ooze back – into the side of my consciousness, because they *just didn't make sense*. It made no sense to see the energy flowing from flower to leaf bud to tree and through me to the blade of golden wheat behind and then flying into the breeze of the clouds above. It made literally zero sense to feel the telepathy with others, to be able to have flashes of what they were thinking and sometimes the future and then have them actually happen, to be able to read what was and what could be every once in a while. And so I told myself that none of that had really happened, I was imagining it, and I stopped trusting my instincts and my intuition and my woman understanding because it just made *no sense*. And then...there I was. Reading it all in a book. Voicing out loud all of the things that had always been calling to me.

That's exactly how it came about with me and the story of Catholicism.

I was raised sort of Protestant. We toodled from Presbyterian to Lutheran to Methodist, pretty much quitting it all once I (the youngest in the family) completed confirmation. And yet...it called to me. While in high school, I took an amazing Humanities class where we basically studied comparative religion, and it was at that point that it came to me – I couldn't *not* believe in something. Not that I believed, at that point, in one of those stories specifically. Indeed, I still learn incredible truths and beauty and wonders from all of the stories of religion because for me, they all contain different facets of that truth. I just realized, at that point, that there was something out there – and it was calling to me to be a part of it.

And so...for me, this thing that's calling to my soul, that's always had that quiet, insistent voice inside of me – I've finally accepted that it's real. And that my life is, in fact, immeasurably better for it. And being a totally selfish human being, that's kind of all that has mattered to me. The logic for me goes: It makes my life better and easier (in the long run...), so

I'm going to do that thing. And my only job is to trust myself enough to accept it. That's it. It's there. All I have to do...is say yes. Because, in the end, that voice is the Captain of my soul, and it's my job to trust myself enough to listen to that Captain. However you tell that story.

My personal story? It's the story that's told by the Catholic church. That's the one that gets me. And that, in the end, is why I don my breastplate of protection every morning. That's why I go to mass on Sunday and wake every morning at 5 am to journal with the Christian God. It's not because I think everyone should follow the same beliefs that I do. Good Lord the world would be so very boring if we were all the same. It's because I've found that life is *hard*, y'all. And finding the strength to keep saying yes takes every minute of conversation with my Captain that I can squeeze out. Because church every Sunday fills me with strength – or needles me with the necessary pokers to get moving where the Universe needs me, even when I don't want to go. Because I need a constant reminder that I've chosen to don a cape and Superwoman boots. Because this story, the story that I like to read over and over, voices out loud all of the things that I've always known deep in my soul, even if they don't make any sense at all. The story of love and redemption and really, really messed up people being forgiven and given another chance and strength and calling out the crap that is really going on in the world and fighting for what I believe in. It's a story that sings to my soul. And that, in the end, is for me the whole point.

So that's my story. And it is most certainly not everyone's. I love love the stories from one of my dearest friends of the

Hindu gods. And the Buddhist stories – as do the Shinto, from our time in Japan – bring incredible peace and calm to my spirit. I love love the Mormon sensibility of community, and the Christian Science strength of the love over the darkness. All of those stories have helped me so much. Along with the stories of women that have also suffered from bulimia, survivors of abuse and betrayal. All of those stories have made me feel not so alone, have helped me realize that I am not alone in all of these crazy situations and what seem like inappropriate feelings. The stories help me to accept myself as I am, and sometimes give guidance on what other people have done to help overcome during their fire-walks.

Sooooo...if I had something to say here, it would be to tell your stories. Because all of the other superwomen out there? We need them. Because stories give us strength. Stories help us to stand together. Stories help to make sense of it all. At least they did for me. In the hardest times of my life, it's been the stories of others that have helped me maintain my sanity. And, I think...there's something about finding the story that works best for you. And accepting all of the weird, mystical, crazy-ass things that we often feel but that don't make any sense, and realizing that other people have felt those same things through all of eternity. Because this Universe is just one big ball of mystery and wonder, and I've found that the more I accept that to be true, the more the Universe gives me in return. Definitely one of the strengths of the Superwoman.

Chapter 13

IMAGE 3.0 –
MARATHON CEO EXTRAORDINAIRE

A few years ago an article appeared in *Esquire* that has now become a famous reference point for people interested in how gender affects interactions in society. And while it's full of many nuggets of goodness, the golden nugget that stuck out the most to me was the reference to a study on how much women don't get to talk. And I know. Stick with me here.

Basically this study put together a couple of groups of men and women, assigned a topic to discuss, and gave the women different instructions (the men were in the dark). The women in one group were told to speak up and contribute 50% of the time – i.e. exactly the same amount of airtime as the men – as they were contributing ideas to the group. The women in the other group were told to speak up only 20-30% of the time, leaving the extra 70-80% of the talk time to the men. And then they surveyed the men afterward to find their responses to the group. And what came out of it was that, basically, the men in the group of equal-airtime women said that the women in their group were bossy, domineering, overbearing, and not good team players. While the men in the 20-30% women airtime group called those women great contributors, really interesting discussion mates, and effective team members.

Yep.

So, ok, we can go a few different ways with this. And while one of my business partners goes the route of "we need to help the men adjust!" and I *one hundred percent* agree with her and that's on the horizon for our business, I think for me, right now, there's another takeaway. And it's a takeaway that I've learned over many, many years of business and leadership.

She who talks the least in the room is the least influential. *Or* She who talks the least in the room holds the most power of all. *It's your choice.*

So let me explain.

Have you ever been in a group of people that are trying to accomplish something or trying to move forward their own agendas? Often I have found that what happens in that time is that everyone is arguing, talking over each other, stating their own opinions vociferously. And if you take a look around the room, act as the fly on the wall, you will see (at least I have found) that there are always a couple of people that are being quiet and soaking it all in. And while some of those people are the voices that are being unheard in the discussion...some (or at least one) of those people is the most powerful person there – one of those people is the decision-maker. Because (and here's a leadership secret) the best leaders are the ones that are the stupidest ones in the room. And the stupidest ones keep quiet.

Yep. The stupidest ones. Michael Dell quote here: "Try never to be the smartest person in the room. And if you are, I suggest you invite smarter people...or find a different room. In professional circles it's called networking. In organizations it's called team building. And in life, it's called family, friends, and community."

So here's the point: the stupidest people in the room? Those are the ones that sit quietly and take in all of the information. Those are the ones that aren't scared to ask the questions that show that they're the stupidest ones in the room. Have you ever seen this happen? It's an amazing thing to see, superwomen, if you haven't ever done it. Be in a discussion with men. Let's say there's a point that you don't understand. Voice it out to the group. There will be a *cacophony* of voices trying to jump all over themselves to explain it to you, because the people that still haven't learned leadership are convinced that all they have to do is voice the smartest opinions to get the promotion.

Wrongo. Bongo. You want to be a leader in the room? Stay quiet. Sit and listen to everything. Empower the voices that aren't being heard (e.g. *"we haven't heard from Sam in a while, what are you thinking about this, Sam?"*). And sit quietly and think about it. Multitask in your brain (something women are really good at). Pull together all of these odd different ideas, and summarize it succinctly. And then ask questions to get to a decision.

Ohhhh, it gives me goosebumps to think about it. All this time, we've been bemoaning our lack of airtime, when in fact

it *really* just means that when we say something, *it's important.*
People stop to listen.

And they only stop to listen if they perceive you as a power
source.

Ok, so here's where we get to the crux of the image part.
And this is what I've learned up to this point. Men, at some
point in history, all got together and said "So, it's trousers?
Yep. Trousers." and they gave up the power that comes with
differentiated clothes and our individuated image. Because
men got on the train that we should all look the same in order
to maintain power, whereas women realized that *image is an
incredible opportunity to demonstrate our power*. And that,
sister-friends, has made all of the difference.

A few years ago, Annette – a fellow superwoman – talked
me into doing a marathon. And it wasn't just any marathon. It
was the Great Wall Marathon. As in one of the hardest
marathons in the world. And while I didn't know that at the
time, I found that out at about the 5:30 mark, when we had to
climb back *up* on that Wall in the Himalayas and my thigh
muscle cramped and I said to myself "I've pushed out babies
with no drugs, this is *not* going to break me" and, yes, we fin-
ished it. There was most definitely crying at the end. And it
was from that point on that I have claimed marathoner as a part
of my image. And do you know how I did that? I looked at
Annette and my sister (another runner extraordinaire) and figured out what they looked like that made people realize that

they were runners. What did their bodies look like? What kind of clothes did they wear? How did they move their bodies? And then I started doing the same – because I saw that people have immense respect for marathoners and, in many cases, think that they can do anything they set their minds to. Because, pretty much, they can (I can say this now with 9 marathons under my belt). And I want people to know that about me the moment I enter a room, before I've uttered a word.

And then I started my own company, and I realized that I needed to *look* the part as well as act it if anyone was going to take me seriously. And so I literally drew – yes, drew (terribly I might add) – the image of myself in my journal as that multinational CEO that I wanted to become. *And then I made it happen.* Because, just like we all need parents to look up to to figure out what the heck we're supposed to do in this world, we need images and figures to look up to to accomplish any goal that we want. I think maybe that's why we love models and actors so much in our society – because they give us a literal image to strive for, to show the world and ourselves that it is possible, and that is who we are.

And so now, every time I leave my house, I know that I will have less talk time than men. And knowing that I want to use that as one of my superpowers, I think very carefully about the image that I want to project – because that image will speak for me, before I say a word. That image will either say "I'm a mouse and am a bit afraid to be so awesome" or it will say "This is a badass marathoning superwoman that can take on the world. Sit up and take notice."

Oh, how immensely, immensely grateful I am for this amazing image that is my secret weapon. And yes. It takes a lot of work and time and occasionally tears to keep my body looking this part. And no, for me that does not mean surgery or covering my grays. It means taking the time to take care of myself, and love every single gray hair because *I earned those gray hairs*. And you know what? I don't give a rat's ass if your way of doing it is with surgery and hair dye and botox. I know those women and love them and raise my glass of prosecco to them and say "here's to you, secret superwoman. I see you've found your superpower, too."

Cheers to us, then. Because it's not the devil that's wearing Prada. It's just a bunch of badass superwomen that occasionally throw on that killer look. Sometimes the menfolk just can't tell the difference.

Chapter 14

A LITTLE STORY ABOUT PIRATE DRAGONS

Did you know that all of us have voices inside our heads? Yep. Every single one of us. Research backs that up.

Thank God I'm not the only crazy one here.

In his phenomenal book (read it, no joke) *Positive Intelligence*, Shirzad Chamine outlines his lifelong pursuit in search of these voices – the voices he calls *saboteurs*. Same voices that, 500 years ago, St. Ignatius called "affects and thoughts from the evil spirit" – just not quite so succinctly. We've all got them and apparently humanity has had them forever – and they are Pesky. Little. Beasts.

So imagine that your life is like a river, and you're the driver of your boat (yes, this story has a Garth Brooks soundtrack that goes with it in my mind). So there you are, standing at the tiller, your hands positioned at 10 and 2 and your soul is poised to take on the world. The current of the river is your life purpose, where you're meant to be going. Standing next to you is your Captain, holding up the compass and helping you to find the best path.*

On this boat you also have some other characters – the crewmembers and the pirates. The pirates are there trying to get you off course, knocking holes in your boat, trying to get you to steer into rocks or down the wrong stream. They do all of this by whispering fears and lies into your ear – fears of "I can't ever do that" or "I just need to try harder" or "it's not fair that the world is like this" or "we can *never* do that, it's too dangerous and anyway it doesn't make logical sense." And guess what? Every. Single. Person. Has. Them.

I have worked with people all over the world, from C-suite executives to women in huts in Kenya. We've all got 'em. Shirzad agrees – and he's got 40 years of experience and research backing him up. We all, all of us, have the voices that tell us that we're frauds and everyone is going to find out, that we're not good enough, that we will never be able to achieve that goal because we've always failed in the past.

Darn those pirates.

Fortunately for our fearless boat-driver, we also have a group of characters called Crewmembers. And oh, the crewmembers make all the difference. Crewmembers like, "The One Who Loves You the Most" and "The Listener" and "The Wise Elder From the Dawn of Time." These crewmembers give us all the strength and the courage and the wisdom to choose the right path, get unstuck from the rocks and boulders placed in front of us, and help us to fly with freedom to exotic ports of wonder in the beyond. Yep. The crewmembers are pretty rad.

So here's a secret I'd like to share with you (I've never said this publicly before):

My saboteur pirates are just my crewmembers turned into dragons.

Yep. That's it. There it is. My deep dark secret. And...let me explain.

The conventional wisdom about saboteurs is that the best way to deal with them is first to *know* about them (hence why you should read his book – *life. changing*), and second be able to disassociate yourself from them and dismiss or ridicule them. And yes, in the moment, I've found that to be the best strategy. So when I'm in a meeting or with friends or with my kids and I hear "Shut. Up. You should NOT be saying that. Clearly you don't know what you're talking about and they're going to find out," I've found that an effective practice is to say "Oh, hello pirate Judge, nice to see you," put those words into the voice of Scooby Doo, and move on with what I was going to do anyway.

However, in the long run? In the long run I've experimented and strategized and come to the conclusion that I have to deal with these voices as we have to deal with any other dragon. And the only way to slay a dragon, of course, is to pour waterfalls of love all over it.

Have you ever been in a situation where someone is so *angry* with you that they're spitting fire, pouring out hurt and destruction at every turn? I have. Hellooooo dragon. And I have found that not once, *not once*, did it work for me to cajole them, to be angry at them in turn, to try to reason with them. Which, frankly, sucks, because those are the things that I really want to do and am naturally quite talented at. I've used them a lot – and while those tactics might work in the short run, in the long run those dragons inevitably leak out the edges and come back to pour more fire on top of my head.

Do you know the only thing that's ever worked for me for any period of time? Love. Love. Like, *massive* love in some cases. Love that's unfair, because I had no idea I was hurting people in that way. Love that makes *no sense*, because I was working so hard to make everything right, how dare they be angry at me? Love that is exhausting because *hello I am doing all of the things grow up and deal with it*. Love. Love. Waterfalls and waterfalls of seemingly unearned love.

Same is true with those pirate dragons.

When I'm running around doing all of the above-mentioned ALL THE THINGS and my hyper-achiever saboteur pirate says "you need to do more! More! This is definitely not enough!" I have learned that, when I am rational and have the ability to stop and listen and hear what she has to say, it goes something like this:

"Talk to me, sweet Hyper-Achiever" (I've nicknamed her Miss Busy-Body).

Miss Busy-Body: "I don't know what to do!! I am trying so hard and it never seems to be enough. It's like there's this un-ending list of things and everyone is expecting so much of me and I just can't do it anymore and if I stop I'll lose everything and the world will fall apart and I'll never get to where I want to go and I just *don't know what more I can do* and I don't know the right thing to do and I'm just trying so hard…"

Me: "Whoa, I can see you're so angry…And you know what? I completely understand…You are right to be angry. Seriously. Talk about frustrating and feeling worthless and alone. And…shoot. I'm so, so sorry. Crap. I messed that up. I've been ignoring you a lot, haven't I? Well …nuts. I love you so much, and I haven't been telling you that of late. You are so important to me, and so wonderful, and I see you. I'm so sorry. I haven't been spending enough time with you, have I?"

"Sniff …noooooo….."

"Oh, my fabulous, what an ass I've been. Crap. I'm so sorry. It must be awfully confusing and scary and alone in there, huh?"

"Sob….it *is*. And I don't know what to do! I'm just trying to help and I have no idea what you need and so…"

"Yeah…I hear you. And you are right. It's my fault. I've been so neglectful of you. I am so sorry. Because I love you so and think you are incredible. What can I do to make it better?"

"Well…I mean, honestly? I kind of just want to sit and talk with you. Can we talk about everything we've done together up to now? And just sit and be so proud of how amazing it is? Can we…can we talk about this beautiful life we have built, this incredible world in which we live, the quiet beauty of hearing the birds in the trees on a summer evening? Because…

I mean. We've done pretty well. Like, really well. And I think...
I think maybe just sitting and talking about that and savoring
it might make it better."

Helloo, Appreciator Crewmember.

And so, at the heart of every saboteur pirate dragon within
us lies a crewmember, a piece of myself that I've forgotten
about, not spent enough time with lately. A poor, sweet dragon,
running around trying to do *something* because they haven't
talked to me in ages and they just don't know what to do to
make it better for me. And, frankly, that's their number one job
in life – to make it better for me. Pretty amazing, huh?

Poor lost dragons. All they need is what all of us need, when
we get right down to it. Someone to love us, in spite of our
occasional fire-breathing tendencies.

I invite you to get to know those pirate-dragons. Because
frankly, they tend to run our lives. And if there's anyone that's
running my life, I personally would like to at least talk to them
about where we're planning to go.

*Co-Active Training Institute, *Who Is on Your Crew? (And Why You
Need One!)* https://coactive.com/blog/

THOUGHT QUESTIONS

Chapters 8 – 11

1. Do you have a Captain, oh my Captain? A Lion that has stood with you in your subconscious, helping to place each step? If so, write a bit about him or her below – what is s/he like? If you're feeling stuck, start tapping into Spirit Animals...if this Captain was a Spirit Animal, what would it be? Why? What are the characteristics of that animal that lend it to call to your Spirit?

2. Have you put any layers of paint on over your diamond? If so, what form have those layers taken? If you could give those layers a color, what would they be?

3. What's available for you if you were "unfuckable?" And, if you can tease it out, what's the biggest thing that you tend to judge others on, and feel judgement on in return?

4. If your image throughout life were a rainbow, what would be the colors? How have they changed? Have any of them stayed the same?

Chapters 12 – 14

1. What stories have helped you through your life – "made it all easier, so just accept it"? What stories have made it harder? Sometimes these are the stories that we tell ourselves, hear on repeat in our heads. Often the unhelpful ones turn on at 2 am in the morning. What are a few of them here?

2. What is exciting to you about taking charge of your image? What freaks you out? Why Who is a celebrity/person/fairytale that helps to inspire and/or give you power there?

3. If you could walk into a room and have your image, your aura, declare one thing about you, what would it be? And, in a most perfect world where everything is possible, how would your image declare that – what clothes, etc?

4. Do you know a bit about your personal pirate-dragons that keep you down? How do you tend to deal with them? Do you take charge and stomp all over them? Do you avoid them like the plague until it feels they've disappeared? What works best for you?

PART 3

VOCATION

Chapter 15

VOCATION 1.0 – MILSPO

So, I want to spend a wee bit of time talking about vocations. And because I love breaking boxes and seeing things from new lights, I'm going to talk about slightly non-traditional vocations. For while I started life thinking of vocation as simply the career and profession that one goes to and gets paid for, I've started to realize that some vocations we don't get paid for – even though they are, most assuredly, vocations for real. And I frankly think society should pay us for some of those vocations – for it seems that we most definitely value that work in society. And I get ahead of myself. For now, I'd like to dive into my first vocation – one that really, really didn't look like a vocation when I first took it on.

Remember how I told you about my seven-year-old self, raising my She-Ra sword of power on the front lawn? Well, 15 years later, imagine, if you will, that same girl, standing in front of another tree – a big, arching maple tree filled with the green of mostly-new, not-quite-baby leaves. I stood under this tree, dappled in sunbursts through those cusping adults, in a slightly different shiny outfit, and glowing from the inside out. Across from me was standing the most wonderful, caring man a girl could hope for, replete in a smart and dashing uniform. Fresh out of college, I got married on my childhood lawn to a uniformed officer in the US Army that I had fallen in love with during University. And yes. I am a military wife. Talk about unexpected.

So I grew up in a family of chemistry professors. For anyone that doesn't know, the military and the sciences often duke it out for federal funding – usually if you increase military spending, that means less government money for the arts and sciences. It's the perennial battle of security versus freedom – just how much security do we need to grow the results of a free society, and how much is superfluous?

Having grown up with scientists, you can imagine their views on the matter.

I remember vehement and heated discussions around the dinner table railing against military expenditure increases. This was between detailed expositions on the bending and binding of DNA and TATA boxes. Yep. It was a weird childhood.

So when I happened to fall in love with a military man, there was a *lot* of confusion to go around. Not only that, but he came from a family of military people, so their views on the world and politics were the polar opposite of mine and my family's.

Talk about sparks. I was an environmental economist major that hugged trees and didn't even know what ROTC stood for. Here I was, a hippie child, in love with the environment, an ardent feminist, raised by two chemistry professors, and now promised to marry a man in the military. And clearly, that now meant a whole pile of craziness headed into my life – because we got married shortly after America entered Iraq, and was in the heart of the conflict in Afghanistan. I had *no* idea what I was getting myself into.

And while this tension has kept our marriage incredibly spicy and fiery, it has also created a lot of collateral damage around us. We've watched as our parents have each been pulled more and more fanatically to the opposite sides of the political spectrum, and we've been beaten and berated for standing in the middle. I remember one time in particular when my stepfather called my husband a Nazi for being in the military. He's since apologized (and very well, I might add – he loves my husband so)...and it is still a comment that lives in the in-between. Other relationships haven't been able to withstand the tension, much to our immense sadness, and we've stood by helplessly as some of our most loved ones have drifted further and further to the sides.

When we first arrived in Georgia – our first duty station – we thought we couldn't get an apartment, so we stayed (as part of our honeymoon) in the BOQ, or the Bachelor's Officer's Quarters. And yes, I hear every Army wife out there gasping because ewwwwwwww. It was disgusting and full of bugs and a teeny tiny room – and it was paradise. I remember particularly that my shower-taking was like a flamingo dance – the water temperature fluctuating so wildly over the course of seconds that I had to dodge in and out of the spray to avoid being alternately scalded or frozen. It was a dance more with the walls than the water, and let me tell you – I became an expert *really* fast at that wild flailing rhythm. And yes I meant flamingo instead of flamenco. There was nothing as graceful as the flamenco dance about it.

And it wasn't just the BOQ shower-dance that confused the hell out of me – it was *everything*. Have you ever been taken from your total known comfort zone and plopped into bizarro world? That was 100% my experience in this unknown land. I'd been taken from safe, uber liberal Seattle and University of Washington hippie culture (love you so!) and been dropped on Mars. And it wasn't even just Mars – it was *Martial* Mars. I remember one time in particular when we were first welcomed into a unit and "roasted" at the Hail and Farewell. Expecting a normal, kind welcoming – such as the one a new professor would receive in a chemistry department party in Nebraska – I was completely shattered when, instead, they called my husband and me to the front, found our most embarrassing traits, and died laughing over them. I will *never* forget the humiliation of having my husband called "furry teeth" because we'd been too poor to replace our toothpaste when it ran out the week prior. That knife still twists a bit in my heart when I think about it. And I am forever grateful to them for doing so, because it started forging those bonds of *we can talk about anything together* community, and it started building that iron within myself – both of which I would need as we walked through the fires of repeated deployments together.

Have you ever tried to actually speak with anyone in the military about military things? All of a sudden it's "We need to get the AMP to the FOB in case there's a FRAGO – otherwise we're gonna have a FUBAR."

It's like a completely different language.

So added to my already confusing capability to grasp the intrinsic importance of *having* a military (like, what the heck do they *do* when they're not at war?? Sit in an office and stare at each other all day?) was my total inability to even understand the actual words coming out of my husband's mouth. And do you know what? I thank God for how different we are every day. Because it's given me this space where I could live in the in-between, and break my own self and ideas. It has let me break and create and live and mold together two worlds and stories until something totally new and different has emerged.

That day in late Spring when I stood in my parent's backyard, pledging fealty to this man (and yes, that is completely what that felt like) was the beginning of a new vocation for me – even though I didn't know it at the time. In fact, I vehemently rejected the vocation of "wife" that was thrust upon me – and instead told myself a story of defeat for over a decade. It was the first story I told myself about marriage – and it was a story worth breaking.

Let's set the stage for this story. Remember my tree-hugging, feminist-loving sparks that were just starting to light? Well, I had decided that, right out of college, my first vocation was to join the Peace Corps, move to New York City and live the *Sex and The City* life, enter government policy action and stave off global warming by convincing people of it's hugely negative economic impact.

For a long time, I told myself the story that I had failed in my first vocation. And eventually I blamed it all on this military man. And, oh, that was a story that needed to be broken.

Because what *really* happened in my life was this: that day when I said those fateful words under that tree, I was taking on the full-time job of being a wife.

Sooooo ...having been married for over 15 years now, I can say one thing about that. Being married is *hard*. It is so effing hard. It is literally an at least full-time job to figure out how to make that all work. And it's exhausting. And man, I wish someone had told me that when I first got married – because then at least I could have set my expectations.

For me, I couldn't make this into the part-time job shared between two spouses that many people do now – mostly because my other half was just literally not there to share the job with me. And the main issue for me was that I just couldn't accept it at the time, because *being a wife as a vocation??* Talk about 1950s Stepford-ism.

So this is the story I told myself over and over of how my life went down for the first 10 years of my adulthood: I failed in my personal dreams and instead became the barefoot and pregnant wife to an officer in the military. This was a story I told myself for a decade, and it *tore me apart*. And you know what? It could have been the truth – had I done that first job of wife differently. And yet...looking back on it now, I see a very, very different story – and the drive and intention and perspective with which I tackled that job made all the difference – as it does in any career.

I invite you to turn that periscope around and see if you can spot the new constellation.

My husband deployed a lot. And yes, not as much as others – there are fellow sister-warriors that lived through *eleven* deployments – and yet, for the first eight years of our marriage he was absent for four of them. And just to add more complexity, it wasn't a clean four years – it was four years of in and out, of intense love and ripping agony, of tearing loss and wildly ecstatic reunions, of love that we thought was perfect and agonizing betrayal.

It was a veritable shit-show.

I worked outside of the home for the first one and a half deployments, which helped to give me a bit of the confidence that I was a really good manager and leader. And it also gave me something to do when he was gone, even though it was a disaster to be working when he was home. I remember how incredibly *lonely* it was during those deployments – I would see a car that looked like his driving by on the street and my heart would leap – maybe he had somehow come home? I would save all of his shirts and never wash them and bury my face in their smell to open my heart and feel our love because I might die if I kept cutting it off in self-defense. I remember one weekend in particular, when I had stayed up nights and inhaled whole the *Time-Traveler's Wife* (fyi fellow milspos – that stands for military spouse – *not* a good deployment read), finally coming to the end and curling up into a ball on the landing at the top of the stairs and ripping sobs tearing from my soul as I knew knew *knew* that there was nothing I could do to make it ever stop, that he would always be a soldier leaving me over and over. Not that I would want to stop him from being a soldier, from being *him*, because that is the incredible soul that I had fallen in love with. And oh, that didn't stop the agony of giving ourselves and not really knowing what that cost would actually be.

We married folk are quite the fools, aren't we?

In military spouse preparation land (thank you, soul-sisters) – also known as spouse coffees – they tell you all about the deployments, and how hard they are, and how little you can communicate, and how much it sucks.

What they don't tell you is that it's even worse when they finally do come back home.

Have you ever seen the movie *American Sniper*? My husband and I went to go see it in the movie theatres when it came out. By about five minutes into the opening scene, all of our usual joking and movie-theatre banter had disappeared. By fifteen minutes in, we were no longer allowing our hands to touch as we reached for more popcorn. By the thirty minute mark, neither of us could move or even *think* popcorn. Or, really, even think at all.

It was like watching our life up on the big screen.

Every fight, every argument, every emotion that lived through those characters – they were *our* fights, our words, our anger and hurt and shame and breaking screech of agony that we had lived out in our world as we battled through deployment and coming back home and deploying again.

I remember leaving that theatre and, not being able to look at my husband, breaking the silence by saying "Well. That was weird." And his characteristic one-word response: "yeah."

Remember how I spoke about redeployments earlier? That time of coming BACK from a deployment? They're really hard to explain – and I think they bring to a head the issues that so many of us face in our marriages.

How can I explain redeployments? You know those times in life when you've gone through something really hard, you've walked through a great big fire, and you're still wrestling with the tail end of it to try to figure out what on Earth that *means* – and your spouse is sitting on the couch grunting laughs at Netflix?

Yeah. It's like that.

I remember one redeployment – must have been after the first deployment, as I was driving home from work when this happened – listening to a story on NPR about a family that had gone through a deployment. And what it was like for the spouse who stayed at home. And I excitedly picked up my phone and called my husband and said "I'd really love for you to listen to this program and I'd love to talk about it when we both get home." And his response of "okay." And I remember the rest of that drive, navigating home as excited thoughts raced through my head – so many questions we could ask each other from this! So many good ideas on how to connect and how to *find* each other after this fire we both walked through! And as I ran up the stairs, past the crying landing and into our room, all of my hope and enthusiasm and love crashed to the ground as I found my husband asleep in our bed.

Asleep, y'all. Freaking. Asleep. At 6pm. After I'd just called him and asked for one tiny, teeny thing in an attempt to save our marriage from the morass into which it was sliding.

I didn't talk to him for a whole month.

Later, on another deployment round, I remember driving home and speaking with my sister, and telling her how hard it was to have my husband gone, and how much I missed him. And she, bless her beautiful, amazing, loving heart, said, "You know, I think that my husband and your husband have really similar jobs. I mean, my husband is gone a lot, and leaves me often on my own."

And while my soul chafed at that time that she might be *vaguely* going through what I was going through (her husband is a visual effects editor in Hollywood, my husband was being shot at), do you know what? She was right. She was on her own, struggling to hold it together too. She had to act the single parent – as so *many* of us do, including the married ones, because our spouses travel so much or work so late – so often. And what's more – my husband hasn't had to deploy in years. Her husband is still leaving fairly often to shoot on location. Nobody gets the monopoly on pain and heartache. And no pain is worse than anyone else's.

We're all in this together. And we all experience the same amount of agony and ecstasy. It's what we do with it that matters. So while my wife-vocation story happens to be one of a military spouse, I think it's possible that it has more similarities to other spouse stories than differences.

Do you know what are the top three things married people fight about? Sex, money, and children. And if you want to keep your marriage together, all you have to do is talk – without the

TV, without anything – with each other for 15 minutes a day. That's it. Statistically, if you speak less than 7 minutes a day, you're much more likely to get divorced.

My husband and I have fought about all of those things. We have gone days, months of talking less than 7 minutes a day. I'm guessing that you other married superwomen out there have gone through the same – because love doesn't change just because you speak it in a different language, different time zone, or different political status. Love and marriage are a choice. Just like a job. And when you sign on the dotted line – when you say I do, I will love you to the end of my days, even when you are of zero use to me in any way whatsoever any more – you sure as poop are taking on a leadership role in a whole new company.

My marriage has given me the skills of grit and determination. It's taught me how to budget and give money to the appropriate line items to grow the partnership. I have patience and persistence for *days*, not to mention strategic planning. I know how to develop new initiatives, to pour capital back into the business in order to let it grow, to invest and save for future bumps in the road. I can inspire and motivate people, gain their trust and find their best parts and use them in service to the business with one hand tied behind my back. I know how to organize literally everything. Communication, soft skills, human development? Forget about it. I had those down within the first 90 days.

You want to talk about a vocation? Get married. Go all-in. Make a rock-hard promise that you're stuck with this ridiculous, lovable, super annoying and fantastic person till the end of your days. Trust me, you will gain all the skills necessary to make any successful business run – because it's either that or be stuck with a lump on a log until you die. Marriage is the best apprenticeship to become a leader. You'd be a shoe-in for a job at any company that you'd ever actually want to work at.

Chapter 16

VELOCIRAPTOR CHILDREN

Let me introduce you to my velociraptor children.

I have great kids. Let me stop here and say that. For reals. They're amazing. Through the grace of good friends that have helped me, the Universe that has taken the really hard challenges and stood by my side, and the fire-walks of motherhood, we have created amazeballs little human beings. And they're still velociraptors.

Have you ever seen the movie *Jurassic Park*? Remember how the velociraptors were really the most terrifying of all beasts, because they would constantly, relentlessly, unendingly be throwing themselves against the boundaries of their existence, looking for the weak spots until they could finally break free and eat us all?

Yep. My kids are like that.

I realized this fairly early on in the mom journey – at that point it was called toddler-hood. This was the time in my life when my sweet, wonderful wee little man that called water "baba" and smiled at me sweetly turned into a wild ravening beast that never slept, screamed from his room during naptime, and tried to stab his baby sister in the back with a butter knife. Yep. Velociraptor. And I realized, basically, that these velociraptor tendencies showed the most in my two-year-olds whenever I said no. Because what does every two-year-old do when someone tells them no? *They lose their bacon*. Like, in every way possible. They throw themselves on the floor. They throw anything possible at you. They scream until the neighbors call the cops. They hit as many things possible. Occasionally they pee on themselves, or hold their breath until they pass out. They do themselves bodily harm. They ask you why 10,000,000,000,000,000,000,000 times until you want to rip out your eyeballs and claw at your face and act out every Homeric tragedy you can remember as you drink as much wine as possible to forget it all. Yep.

Velociraptors.

And so...here's the rub. At some point I realized my 2-year-olds were not just serial killers in the making. They were just velociraptors. They were testing the fences. They were throwing themselves against the mile-high, electrified barbed wire, repeatedly. They were ripping off their limbs and throwing it at the boundaries to see if they still stood. They were roaring and shrieking at the gamekeepers as terrifyingly as possible to see if they would run away and leave the switches unoccupied, thus giving the wild velociraptor children the chance to deviously turn them off with a stick that they had fashioned for just such a purpose *Because they wanted to know if they could really, actually trust us as parents*.

Yep. That's it. Because the world is *freaking scary*. And at some point around age two we as human beings start realizing that. We stop thinking that the world is all of us (babies think that) or that there's no such thing as bad and...we start realizing there are crazy things out there. And we look at our parents and are like "soooooo...yeah. Not so sure if you can actually handle all of that stuff. I mean. Who says you're tough enough to actually keep me safe?

Do you remember the story of *Hansel and Gretl*? Hansel and Gretl's parents *let them out* into the scary world. They not only took away the boundaries, the parents themselves took them out there. And Hansel and Gretl, having been there before, were like "no thanks," leaving breadcrumbs behind them. Unfortunately life wasn't on their side, the breadcrumbs being eaten, and Hansel and Gretl are abandoned. And what happens then? Well, the cannibal witch tricks them with sweets and throws them into the oven.

Ummmmm....talk about terrifying.

Kids *need* boundaries, otherwise they just might get eaten up by the world. And you know what? *They know that*. They know that there's a big scary world out there, and they're just not that sure that you can handle it. So they see just how tough you are – just how much you can take. And it's literally our job as parents to put those boundaries around them, protect them, and teach them what works and what doesn't. Eating 3 pounds of sugar? Nope. That doesn't work so well. That's why we say no to that as parents. Never sleeping? Reference torture methods to see if we, as a society, think that sleep deprivation falls on the side of "yes please!" or "possibly the worst thing you can do to a human being." It's *our job* to put up those boundaries and enforce them. Come hell or high water, those little velociraptors need us to say no. And say no *a lot.* Because the more we say no and then actually enforce it, the more they can trust us.

And yet, there's something deeper here. Something that's even more important than just protecting them from themselves and proving your trustworthiness as a leader.

When my son was 19 months old, I undertook the task of potty-training him. Our method was the pantsless pursuit – i.e. nothing on the hinter-regions, allowing him to see immediate cause and effect. And as I was in my first trimester and down for the count with morning sickness, and he is a stubborn little rascal (yep, still is), I decided that that boy could go outside as often as possible so I wouldn't have to clean up as many messes. And as we were living in the barren and cold high deserts at the time, I would clad him in a warm shirt and nothing else and push him out to play. I can still see him now – bare-ass, white-as-a-lily little naked buns flying around in laughter, his gold-and-purple sweatshirt blending in with the brown barren environment surrounding him, chasing our crazy little fluffy white dog with a bucket in his hand, and turning around wildly to have her chase after him in turn, laughter shrieking into the wind behind them both. And I remember, so vividly, him digging into the earth with his little shovel over and over in the barren, brown, dry backyard, having just a teeny tiny postage stamp of an area to play in between the fences, squatting on his little haunches and digging with all of his might to "grow his garden," as he told me – because, frankly, he had nothing else to do.

And isn't that true of all of our little velociraptors? Because when they discover that they have those strong-ass, impenetrable, forever, mile-high fences – when they've thrown themselves against them again and again, exhausted all of their energy in trying to find the weakness and discover that *those boundaries aren't going anywhere* – then, and only then, can they weakly look around and say "well, I guess I should look at this barren earth here and see what I can do with it." Because, when faced with nothing else to do, they can have the freedom and joy and gift to turn to the center...and grow their own garden. And instead of trying to solve all of the problems of the fences, they can turn and solve all of the problems on their insides. They can have the time, and the space, and the safety to discover their own internal garden, to dig and cultivate and explore and try again with something new until they have a huge, lush, amazing rainbow of *themness*, on the inside, that can grow from all of the self-love that they've been able to cultivate.

And, oh, *then* comes the fun part.

Because then, and only then, you will have a teenager on your hands that has this immense, wonderful, fantastic inside garden, and has learned the geography of their inner wonderland. And then you, as the parent, get to play the wizard and magician, and slowly pull back the curtain, and the next curtain, and blow up that section of fence there, and open a gate here. And you get to take away those boundaries and push them out into the forest until they find the witch. Because then, oh then, they'll have the tools to take on the world.

And that's a whole other book.

For now, oh Superwomen, I invite you to become a child again – if only for a little bit. Take some time to cultivate that inner garden. See what it looks like. What flowers do *you* want to grow? What smells, what butterflies, what hedgehogs or prairie dogs are calling out to your soul to be a part of your wonderland? The wonderful news is: you get a choice. You get to choose. What are you going to say yes to? *You* know. It's down there, calling to your soul. And it's simply a choice for you there in front of you – like two platters waiting for your decision. What are you going to say yes to? Because, in the end, what we say yes to makes all the difference.

Chapter 17

VOCATION 2.0 – MOM

My daughter was molested by one of her babysitters when she was four years old.

Yep. It's about to get real, sister-friends.

Due to a certain sequence of events – and us having a *long* discussion with our kiddos around "If someone tells you to *not* tell Mom and Dad something, you run away from them as fast as you can," our wee little 6-year-old butterfly was able to unlock herself and tell us about what had happened.

It was, truly, the only time in my life when I felt like jumping off a cliff. And, as you know, I've been through quite a lot of poop.

You see, I didn't come by this parenting thing very naturally. I remember my sister, who is possibly the *most* natural mother on Earth, seeming to breeze through the first stages of motherhood while I was flopping around like a dead fish.

FYI, being a parent is *hard*. It's *effing* hard. It's one of the hardest jobs I've ever had. And, in my humble opinion, it's the most undervalued.

I decided, shortly after my pregnancy test showed a plus, that I was going to quit my job. Possibly not the best thing for my long-term mental health, and looking back I wouldn't change that decision for the world. I was in an organization with a toxic leader, I was far from home, and I had a husband that was deploying every few months.

And more than that, I had a quest.

In leadership circles people are now talking about quests – what are the quests that each of us, individually and together, undertake to express our own life purpose and make an impact on this world. Quests must involve outside resources, engage and/or lead others, have meaning and impact, and have a specific, measurable outcome.

From the moment my firstborn entered the world, my children were my quest.

Do you know what I'm talking about? It was that overwhelming sense of responsibility, of "I made small people, and it is my job to raise them to be good, contributing members of society." It is this *huge* moment from that first feeling of a fluttery hello inside of you when you realize, oh *crap*, I am insanely responsible for every decision I make regarding this little life because they're too vulnerable and small to make those decisions for themselves.

And y'all. I *sucked* at it.

Like, I royally stunk at it. My poor oldest child...such an experimental baby. My husband always jokes that, with the first one every decision is either Harvard or Alcatraz – you feed them the "wrong" first food – means they're going to Alcatraz.

I was convinced for years that our oldest child was going to Alcatraz.

This is not because he's a bad child, peeps. In fact, he's possibly the most amazing young man I've ever met. Nope, this is because I felt like I was a *terrible* mom – and dangit, I was failing on my quest.

Not sure if I've said this before, but I am very pigheaded and determined. And I have a (sometimes detrimental) hyper-achiever streak. Failure wasn't an option. Especially on a quest as important as this.

And then...there's this other side of it. And that is this: I am not a great person when I'm tired. It's like all of my creative and life juices get decapitated and roll off down the hill. And when I'm really tired, it's like all of my *everything* gets decapitated – and all that's left is an angry, frothing mess.

This came home to me most vividly after the birth of my first son.

Motherhood is a bone-drenching kind of tired that has not existed for me in any other area of my life. And yet here I was – I had been given one of the most amazing gifts I have ever received. It was the gift of a diamond, a deep, deep blue diamond, sparkling with quiet brilliance, a diamond that held depths that could never be reached, not with the most persistent love-gazing. This diamond was wrapped up in the cushioning and safety of a beautiful, healthy wee man – a complete package that stole my heart forever.

At the same time, the universe handed me one of the hardest, most terrible, most awful trials of my life, a trial with which I would struggle and yearn to break free from and hate with all my might because I felt like I was the deepest failure and could never do anything right.

Welcome to motherhood.

Oh, and that feeling of overwhelming, helpless love for my wee man? It took at least 4 months to make it there. *Four Months.* Doesn't sound long unless you've lived through it.

You know that bone-drenching, soul-sucking tired of motherhood? The tired that is all the more terrifying because you can *never* escape it? The tired that goes on and on and on, even when you're weeping on your knees and screaming for it to *just stop already because you can't take it anymore*?? And then...it keeps going, and you realize that you *have* to take more?? That tired. That tired that sees you there and *still* never gives up, relentless in its pursuit to destroy everything that is good and whole about you. The tired that is ever more hideous because you know in your soul that you can't give into it because this little person will die if you do, and that is literally an unthinkable thought, despite any death that you yourself might be going through at the time.

It's the relentless, sucking black pit of tired – oh, tired doesn't even begin to cover it – that christens each new mother into the sisterhood.

I want to be clear here. I do not want to exclude any woman from this story, because I know many a woman that has desperately wanted children and has suffered, in silence and agony, the void that is felt there. Having lost one of my daughters, I know that void – and the quiet scream of soul shattering that comes with it. To you, my sisters, I break my heart. You are with us in the sisterhood as well, christened with unrequited pain.

I once heard that, in Korea, you do not leave your bed for three months after having a baby. That your mother-in-law comes, taking complete care of the baby except its feeding, while you lay wrapped in a seaweed body-cast to regain your girlish flat tummy.

My elephant-belly is a fair testament to exactly how zero percent of that happened to me. And honestly? I wouldn't have it any other way. Because, of course, no story lives in isolation.

The fire-story of my son's first four months was one of me falling in a heap on the floor as a puddle of tears during my attempts to sleep-train that wee man to accept something, *anything* longer than a 15-minute catnap. It was flashes of me wanting to poke my eyes out, of fears of my baby dying because of my incompetence as a mother, of waves of guilt and shame for my terrible, rebellious, non-equipped self that just wanted to *be alone*. And the terror of also being so alone in all of this, feeling like I was the only one of all the new mothers that I knew that just had not one clue on how to do this. I remember one day when my son was about nine months old, my sister – whose firstborn was the same age as mine, and who was and always will be the goddess of motherhood in my eyes

– turned to me and said "this is so *effing hard!* I had no idea it would be like this when I had him" and I almost fell over, weeping with relief to know that I wasn't alone.

And then, when I found out about my daughter, I fell apart even more. And I *couldn't talk* about it with anyone for quite some time, which broke us even more. Oh, yes, we had the therapist to help her understand and somewhat heal. And it was still terribly isolating and *helpless-ing* and frustrating. Because it was my job to raise them and love them and protect them. And I just constantly felt like I was failing them, over and over.

The fire-story was real, and singed a brand on my soul that can never be taken away. It broke me in the core of who I am, and cost me almost every piece of myself to climb back out again.

And yet – failure wasn't an option. You see, I had looked 20-30 years into my future. And I had seen an incredible, close, loving relationship with each of my amazing children. And I had seen a family that supported each other and championed each other and hung together with each other as we grew and grandbabies arrived and we each went out and conquered more quests as we went forth into the world.

I had seen our beautiful future. And I knew that I wasn't going to get there on my own.

I'd like to let you in on something that will explain a bit of why this was such a revolution for me: I'm from Nebraska, y'all. We don't ask for help from others. Nor do we, honestly, talk about our troubles. Like, ever. It's just our job to drive on and figure it out on our own. And while this self authority is fantastic and one of the pillars of leading your own life...it's also one of the first lessons of life to ask for help when you really need it. And I was *really* not good at figuring out how to do that when I was in need.

Not exactly super helpful to a new mom, that.

When the world had finally beaten me down so much that my marriage was falling apart (time #1), three months into this parenting journey, and my brother and sister flew out in an intervention to tell me that I needed to change, I finally cried uncle and laid down my weapons and tapped out of the game. And in the losing, in the tapping out and admitting defeat, I found an incredible power source that I'd been shutting out the whole time.

I found the power of the collective.

Do you know how *incredibly* helpful moms and dads are for each other?? When we're not judging each other (oh, sister-friends, we have to work on that), and we start getting curious, we are the most amazing group of people in the world.

And so I asked all the questions. I became the stupidest mom in the room, and I asked everyone around me for help. Very specifically, I would find the moms that had mastered something in their children – the mom of the super courageous child, for example, or the mom of the squared away teenage boys – and I would ask them *how they did that.* I would poke and I'd prod and I'd dig deep to try to find the nugget of information.

At the same time I was unconsciously working a *lot* on myself. And on how the crap I was supposed to lead this band of ragamuffins that I was creating.

My sister told me, shortly after the birth of our daughter, that I just needed to be the charismatic leader that the kids would *want* to follow, and everything else would work itself out. And I realized in that moment that, no matter how many good tips and strategies I had at my disposal, if I didn't know myself and love all of the awesomeness and frailties of that self, my children would not only eventually stop following me. I realized that, if they didn't have a leader they wouldn't even know where to *go* – and would eventually have not one clue to find their own diamonds.

Hello, superwoman.

It really was from that moment on that I finally accepted the cape and boots that life was handing to me. And it's taken me years to figure out what that really means.

The fire-story started abating after about four months – when kiddo numero uno started eating solid foods and we all started sleeping (I'm telling you, to this day I am a fire-breath-ing dragon if I haven't had enough sleep) – and that's when the love-story started. It took me about four months to really start loving this little bundled diamond, and I fell madly, deeply, hopelessly in love with his brilliance. It is a brilliance that I thank God for every day, and that I can almost not get enough of soaking up. I remember one day, shortly after this love-fall happened, when I called my Mum to tell her about this revelation – this indescribable, soul-flipping, bottomless flight of love. And I realized at some point that she, too, had had this same feeling for *me* – and I was awed to the point of breathlessness. I remember trying to express my gratitude to her over the phone, and hearing her mom-smile as she said "of course, sweetie. It's what we mothers do."

My love-fall has never abated. In fact, it has grown exponentially with each one of our children – isn't that so odd? I still find it a miracle that love can grow so incredibly much. Each child has their incredible uniqueness and grace – my daughter with her steel-tipped butterfly soul, able to both dance a flutter and withstand incredible pain at the same time. My youngest with his soul on fire for love, hugging anyone and everyone and seeming to understand much better than all of us how truly that is the answer to everything. My oldest that I still thank silently – and occasionally openly – for agreeing to be the first one in our family, with his depths and tolerance and brilliant thoughtfulness that leaves me breathless. I am forever indebted to all of my children for sharing that brilliance with me for a short time.

My sister recently told me about some of her time in Australia, and how the whole family had visited an island that was one of the most interesting places she'd ever been. Because this island, while seemingly normal from the outside – with standard beaches and vegetation around the exterior – contained a very remarkable and idiosyncratic center of sand dunes – sand dunes that, in one area, received (for no explainable reason) the most lightning strikes of any place on earth. Lightning strikes that burned together the pieces of sand they struck, leaving behind remnants of new creations. And the dunes, apparently empty and ordinary, displayed, with a little bit of digging, the most beautiful array of different-colored sand – from bright red to deep blue to purple to black, all just under the surface.

A more perfect analogy for each of us superwomen I could not find. Seemingly normal on the outside, forged with fire and new creation on the inside, and deep deep deep with the vibrant colors of our individuality just beneath the surface.

Such is what I've learned in motherhood.

What a waste of a vocation, eh? Yes, society derides so deeply this vocation – much to our peril.

Can I tell you something else? Parents that *do* it – that really take up that mantle and walk through the forging fires of parenting small people – y'all *they make new life.*

Tell me another job title that can claim the same. CEO? Maybe. Entrepreneur? I've been both – and my thoughts are, if you're successful and do it without any outside capital, perhaps. Anything else? I can't think of another job title that does the same.

And, I am *not* judging. I am *not* saying that any of the other jobs aren't just as important as being a parent. I've *been* those other jobs, I've known how incredibly, incredibly important each one is in creating the fabric of our society, of the future the universe is calling forth, in making this great masterpiece that we are all working on together that we call humanity. Each thread, each needle, is *so* important, and needs to exist and be in exactly the spot where it is playing.

I'm just saying that being a parent is just as worthy of a vocation. And we should recognize it as such.

In a world where the average length of stay in a company is 18 months, parents are tied to a position that lasts 18 *years.*

And this position doesn't pay you – in fact, it sucks all of the money out of you. Talk about learning grit and perseverance. Looking for an employee or leader with grit, perseverance, and ingenuity? Hire a person that's stayed home with their kids for the past 5, 10, 15 years – good Lord, we can talk about grit. Want someone that can motivate insubordinate employees, create new programs and projects that move the company forward with no help from management (because, hello, there *is no management* for parents. Other than begging pleas to God), want someone that can listen to problems and identify good solutions, while also empathizing with the problems? Hire a stay-at-home mom or dad. You will never find someone that is more qualified in leading from all angles of leadership.

And so, for eight years, my children were my quest. They were – and continue to be – the hardest trainers, the most demanding taskmasters, the most call-you-on-your-ridiculousness managers ever known. And this, my friends, is not because we let them rule in the house. No, this is because we pay attention to them, because we throw every part of our beings into helping them along the path, because we enforce tough discipline (definitely the hardest part of being a parent) and make them call us sir and ma'am and hold their toes to the fire and don't let them avoid the fire-walks that life has presented to them. And we walk through those fires with them with insane waterfalls of love, and at the end of the day we collapse on the couch and start drinking our wine with our friends and one of our children does something naughty and every part of our beings are screaming to *just let me relax* and we still, *still* get up off of our tired, exhausted behinds and make the correction that is needed because *they need us* and we brought them forth into this world, and that means that it is one billion percent our responsibility to teach them all of the things that they need – and most especially the rules of discipline and love. Of course, those rules must start from inside – and, oh, that might be the hardest part of all.

Of course, there is another story of parenthood that is possible – because parenthood is a choice. And, with all situations, we have the ability to choose among the choices that are laid out in front of us. I also have walked a very different choice, a different story of motherhood – and the consequences therein.

Can I tell you my other mom story?

I don't think there is a woman on Earth that has ever thought "this child will be loved and adored, taken care of and have the best of everything, and will grow to be a strong, wonderful, cherished member of the community" – and then decided to have an abortion. It's just... not how it goes. And so this argument of when life begins – at conception or after – is completely moot. It is, in my opinion, a red herring, a rabbit down a rabbit hole that takes us into a path of more and more science and theories, and never gets us to the end point of a helpful, thoughtful, loving discussion on the matter.

I've had an abortion. I know of what I speak.

And for my fellow Catholic friends, or anyone else that might be deciding to stop reading this right now, I get it. Totally. And...I invite you to stay. Because, dangit, we need your voice in this. So desperately. I invite you to come with me and explore this aspect of motherhood as well… Because, for me, together is the only way that we'll actually find the way.

I had an abortion about ten years ago – and yes, it's taken me that long to openly talk about it. Ten years ago my husband and I (yep, I was married) were blessed, incredibly blessed, with a third child, a beautiful little girl, one that we had longed for with all of our hearts and souls, a daughter that we have always felt would make our family complete. And…it all went wrong. At nineteen weeks pregnant, we learned that she had no kidney function. And our world came tumbling down.

So, here's what we learned. When an unborn baby has no kidney function, she is unable to make her own amniotic fluid. Since our little June-bug wouldn't have that crucial amniotic fluid, she wouldn't be able to practice breathing in the womb. Since she couldn't practice breathing, her lungs would never develop. And so, when she was born, she would come into this world and gasp and struggle and look at me, her mommy, her protectress, with terrified eyes, and slowly be strangled to death by her own inability to breathe in this world.

I am a lioness with my babies. The thought of this still fills my eyes with tears and helpless terror.

And so my husband and I, after many, many terrible tears, decided to protect our beloved daughter by aborting the pregnancy then, choosing to allow our sweet little June Elizabeth to live her whole life surrounded by our love and strength, instead of making her suffer and live in fear and pain.

It is a choice that, ten years later, I would not make now.

For so long, I would always challenge my unseen critics (those inside my head) with this question: if your child was hooked up to life support, and you *had* to choose between letting her go peacefully in her sleep versus watching her strangle to death, what would you choose? And for me, at least, this was the most terrible, terrible choice, one that I would probably reject if given this hypothetical, saying "well I just can't choose that." No one can. That's the point. It's an impossible situation.

And yet, it's the one in which I found myself. And you know what? Ten years later I've come to the now-understanding that it's not, in fact, the right question to be asking. Because before I aborted my daughter, I had no idea- none, zero, *not one* – of how it would go. No one ever talked to me about it. So. I'm going to talk about it.

Every day after I lost my baby girl I felt the incredible, speechless emptiness of not having her in my arms. I cried every day – *every day* – for a year after she was gone, through the birth and the holding and the loving of a new baby, a son, our much much loved Dean Bean. I cried as I was rocking him to sleep, nursing him and feeling him tug at my heart, because *she wasn't there with us too*. I have followed her through her growth, I know exactly what she looks like and how old she is now, the developmental milestones she's checking off, the ways she would be driving me slightly crazy and the ways she would be creeping even farther into my heart. My heart carries around the burden and the blessing of my June-baby, as it does for each of my children, and I still, still, still beg her forgiveness for the choice I made.

Yep. I do. Dangit, I do, every single day.

I plead silently inside *I'm sorry, baby. I'm sorry I'm sorry I'm sorry. I'm sorry that I made that decision out of fear, out of the fear of having to hold you and watch you die and not being able to fix it all for you. I didn't know that there would always be the 'what if.' What if the doctors were wrong. What if you were a miracle, as my friend's daughter – born when you should have been born – was? What if you were meant to be here on Earth, even for such a short time, to touch the hearts and hold together the web in the way that you were meant to hold it together? I'm terrifyingly, lonesomely, heartbreakingly sorry that I never let you live your what-if. That I never let us live it together. That I didn't have the courage that you needed from me as a mom to stand with you in your struggle, to look in your eyes and hold you and just be with you in the pain and whisper "I know, baby girl. Sometimes it's all warmth and love wrapped around you, and sometimes it's scary and hard. And that's ok – because isn't it, in the end, a beautiful, beautiful life, even through those fire-walks? You're doing such a good job. Your mommy loves you loves you loves you, with all of her might, and I will struggle through this with you because we were made to do this together."*

I never got to say those words to my daughter. Never. Ever. And oh, it has torn my heart to shreds for a decade. Not because I was necessarily wrong in my decision. But because I wasn't necessarily *right* – if that makes any sense at all. And I have a feeling that my heart will be torn to shreds for the rest of my life – even as I'm surrounded by love love love and my ever-wonderful family. Because...she had a what if. And now I'll never know what it was.

And so that, for me, is the bigger argument to have. The discussion we all are invited to open our hearts to. Because, for me at least, it's not a question of when life begins. It's a question of how life is *lived*. And there are, sadly, just some choices that we make that we can't understand until after they are irrevocably made. Decisions that, in the moment, seem exactly and totally like the logical, the best, the most right decision to make given the terrible circumstances. Decisions that only our elders understand, only the people that have been there and loved through it and are not judgemental and don't force their opinions or their stories or their *anything* upon us, just share their stories and say "my love, it is your right to choose. And these are my words."

So what I've found from this parenting journey is that there are many different paths to take. We can choose to be the charismatic leaders that the Universe is calling us to be. Or we can choose to prioritize other things over our children, and let them figure it out without help from us. We can choose to say yes to the terror and the fear that comes with parenting with love. And we can also choose to say no, to say that we're not ready yet, that we need some more time to do it. And you know what? *100% of that is ok in my book.* In fact, 100% of that has actually been lived out in my book. I think it's mostly the awareness of our choices that gives us power – because then we can choose to make the choices that work the best for us.

And so, sister-friends, I invite you to join me in this dialogue. What are your feelings about it? What are your thoughts on motherhood, on parenthood, on choosing and not choosing? How has it worked out for you while you're in the midst of it, and how has it worked out afterwards? I don't know – what is it for you? Because dialogue – real, true, loving dialogue that lets us see into each other's hearts, not each other's fears and hatreds – is what I so desperately wished I'd had access to throughout my whole parenting journey. And let me tell you something else – ain't nobody got the right to take that choice away from you. Because we all get to make our choices – it's just the consequences that happen after that might suck. That's the blessing of free will – it's your choice. The curse, of course, is knowing which choice to make. May we all help to be a beacon for each other in the darkness.

Chapter 18

DRAGONS

This is a story about a powerful and successful woman of the world trapped around a lost girl afraid to see the truth. This is a story about loss and redemption and freedom and dragons. But most importantly, this is a story about truth as we see it. I hope it's not too much for you.

Many years ago in a land far away our heroine embarked on her journey. She carried with her in her pack all of the things she would need – brains to solve any problem, pigheaded determination to persevere, hope and joy and love to see her through. She also carried a few rocks along the way – rocks of past hurts that she pretended weren't there, rocks of self-doubt and fear she'd never make it. And the rocks weighed down her pack – but not more than she could handle.

Our heroine struck forth and walked bravely upon her path, confronting each new dragon as it came to block her way. She traveled all around the world, from Georgia to Hawaii to Japan, working to free others. She worked with nonprofits and governments and military members on three different continents, and she realized something amazing while doing so –

We're all just the same.

She saw other heroines and heroes around her, slaying their dragons and carrying their packs. And she realized that sometimes the rocks in each person's packs became too heavy to bear, and they fall under the weight. And the sight of this hurt her so, but she was too busy fighting her own dragons and carrying her own rocks to know what to do.

And then one day she was handed a rock too big to bear. And she fell.

The rock was in the form of a much-loved, oh-so-longed-for baby girl that left the world before her mom was ready to say goodbye. And our heroine fell under this rock and wept under the weight of it. She shut her eyes to everything around her and ran and ran and ran in circles, desperately seeking for the ladder out. Mercifully, lovingly, and oh-so-tenderly, the rock was lifted and our heroine looked up to see an older heroine, reaching down and giving her a hand.

She was an older woman, a neighbor she barely knew that stopped on her journey to watch our heroine's two older children while our heroine said goodbye forever to her daughter. And this wise, wise woman gave her a gift – she gave her the gift of love and hope and courage wrapped up in a bowl of chicken soup. And when our heroine came home from the hospital and smelled that chicken soup, it felt like...home. And she knew she hadn't lost it all.

This feeling was so amazing that our heroine decided that *this* was what she needed to do – this was her new path! So she started running from hero to heroine and back again, picking up their rocks while still carrying her own. It was exhilarating! To see their faces and hear their new-found hope! No longer did our heroine care about anything else – she was too busy lifting rocks. And yes, ok, these rocks were heavy, but she could do it all! She was stronger than others! This *was* her path!

And when Ebola hit the world, she was right there, ready to heave some rocks into oblivion. She contacted organization after organization, telling them about all of her expertise in lifting rocks. She had run a nonprofit at the tender age of 24. She had built community engagement programs within government and military communities for years. She knew how to grab rocks and make it happen! She was their gal!

And they all – all of them, 100% – came back and said "just give us money. We can lift the rocks better than you."

And then, ohhh, our heroine got mad. Oh, she got so mad. Here was a dragon, right in front of her, lifting everyone else's rocks and telling the heroine to back off. The bastard. How dare he. He was taking all of the joy of lifting rocks for himself and not sharing.

She HATED not-sharers.

So, our heroine decided to do something about it. She decided to fight this dragon and start her own company, one that would help organizations build programs to allow other heroines to lift rocks, and to also encourage – no, convince – those other heroines that rock-lifting was where the real work was to be had. And she fought that dragon, and he just sat there and laughed at her feeble little stabs, picking up rocks and laughing as our heroine battled harder and harder. And as she battled this dragon, other dragons came to fight her on each side – dragons of betrayal by family members, dragons of the worst kind of hurt from her own partner in life, dragons of a lifelong wound to her sweet daughter that was here on earth still. And with each dragon came more rocks – rocks of self doubt, of self hatred, of shame, of guilt.

And did our heroine despair? No! She kept on fighting, more and more and harder and harder, all while still picking up other people's rocks. And in her battle she decided that maybe, just maybe, she just needed to tell people *better* exactly how to fight.

So our heroine found a guide, a wise and trusted advisor, and went to sit at the feet of the master. And she sat and said "I'm ready to learn." And the very first thing that the master said was "lesson number one: you cannot help people by telling them what to do. You cannot be a problem-solver."

"What?" said our heroine. She literally almost quit, one day in. "Solving problems is *what I do*. I don't think this path is for me."

Fortunately, her pigheaded determination came to her aid, and she decided to grind it out, just to say that she had learned from the best.

And then. She fell.

On the second day of training, the master said "come up and practice in the open." Our heroine, supremely confident, came to the front. And she gave it all she had, trying to get the other student to the clear solution that of course was the best and only solution (because our heroine had come up with it). Except...this other student didn't see it! So our heroine tried harder to make her see it. Nope. Our heroine, convinced that this other student was really just stupid (forget that creative resourceful and whole business, people need their rocks lifted!!) just tried harder. She would open her eyes! She would make the student see! And then everything would be solved!

Not so much.

Our heroine failed. And the biggest dragon threw a rock on top of her.

And there our heroine stayed. And because she is who she is, she practiced her sword-fighting under that rock. And slowly, slowly, slowly the sword-fighting shifted. It moved. It was something...different.

And as she sat there under the rock, listening to the master speak the words of truth, she stayed in that dark place. Alone. And sometimes it was really dark. And sometimes it was really lonely. And sometimes she had to lay down her sword and cry and cry and cry for all of the wounds the dragons had inflicted on her. And cry. And cry.

And she realized while she was crying under the 10,000-pound weight of that rock that...she was not alone. She had always been afraid of the rocks, hated them really, because they got people stuck. And now she realized that sometimes you need to be under that rock – and take the voice of the master with you. In fact, that rock, too, can be a part of your path. And as she realized this, the under-the-rock place was no longer quite so dark. There started to grow a light around her. And as the light grew, she realized that there were people down there with her – other heroines, her loved ones, and yes – there were even people *inside* of her, her protector and her Spice Girls and her Saucy Cowgirl. And she was more because of them – and so were all of the people around her. And as the light grew, she realized there was a *whole new path* here. No one needed to lift her rock and pull her out, because *this* was her path. Her new path. Peopled with dragons and rocks, yes – and also with her sister- and brother-hood.

And so, our heroine strikes out again. But this time she does not strike out alone. She strikes out on her own path to empower the amazing females that are out there to change the world – because that is *her* path. And she also knows that, occasionally, she'll need to toss one of the rocks to another warrior or warrioress, and that they'll be there to catch it. And she will need another fighter to stand with her with the dragons – not to fight them, no, never again. Because, you see the dragons were not really dragons. Nope. They were nothing of the kind.

These dragons were, in fact, heroes and heroines trapped inside the wrappings of a person that is afraid to tell the world their truth. These fire-breathing dragons are simply our heroes and heroines that have swallowed their rocks in an attempt to survive. They are the warriors and warrioresses that have seen that, in order to survive, you must make the rocks disappear, pretend they're not there, put on the suit of success at all costs.

Being a recovering dragon, our heroine knows this story well.

This was a story about a lost dragon trapped inside a successful woman, fighting alone to carry and eat all of the rocks of the world. This is now a story about a beaten and bruised and powerful woman, wrapped in the love of a world that only demands that she stands with them. And that, of course, will always be so much more than, and merely, and no more than enough.

Chapter 19

VOCATION 3.0 – MULTINATIONAL CEO

Quite a few years ago, I came face-to-face with someone in this world telling me that there was nothing I could do – there was nothing of value that I, little old stay-at-home mom me could give to this world that was in great need. And let me tell you something, sister-friends. I got *mad*. I got righteously pissed at the injustice of the world telling me that, just because I wasn't born rich or had become a movie star by the age of 23 or because I wasn't *one of them* – you know, those people on TV that just seem so "up there" – that I wasn't good enough, that I didn't have the skill sets needed to really actually help, to leave the real change up to the leaders and the experts and the "people up there" – that, in short, I was expendable.

Oh, I was so *pissed*.

And the fire of that righteous indignation carried me pretty far – it got me to the place where I started my own business to figure this out, I came up with a dream where I could actually connect people in need with regular, everyday people that wanted to help and wanted to do so in their way, in the way that sang to their hearts. And I formed my business, and found an amazing business partner, and gathered advisors and came up with at least a few good ideas on how to move forward.

And then I ran smack into the biggest elephant in the room – the fact that I, myself, had no faith that my own special skills were, in fact, anything very special.

And that's where I remained, stuck with my own apathy and disbelief, as I struggled as an entrepreneur for four long, long, long years.

During that time I accomplished a *lot* in making my business skills grow. I'm pretty sure that, somewhere in there, I had the deep thought that maybe, maybe if I just tried hard enough and got better enough they would want me. Or, maybe, that I would bring something valuable to the world. Because, clearly, as a full-time volunteer, occasional government contractor, and mostly stay-at-home mom, I had proven that I had absolutely nothing to give the world except extreme diapering abilities.

Complete rubbish, that. And there I was.

I read everything I could get my hands on about business. I started getting my MBA. I built upon my experience as a Director of Operations of a nonprofit (pre-baby job) to figure out how to find the most amazing charities in the world.

And then I told other people to go help them.

Yep. Other people. Not me. Not little ol' me. I wasn't good enough yet for that. Not shiny enough.

And then...I found some guides. And they helped me to see the world in a different way. And oh, that made all the difference.

You see, I saw that I had developed so *many* skills in my two previous vocations – that of wife and mother. I saw that, through walking through those fires with integrity, honesty, and immense love, I had learned the lessons of grit and perseverance and leadership and management and everything that all of us that have lived life know is true and everything that I've already outlined.

And this truth set me free.

Do you remember the stories that I told myself for so long about how I had failed? How I hadn't listened to the siren song and had thus given up my dream? Oh, sister-friends, how *wrong* I'd been! No, instead, I'd been on the path, in the boat, tied to the mast and going through the agony, killing the cyclops and defeating the foes, and by coming through on the other end I had *so much more* to give to the world. So much. Like, world-changing much. And that's exactly what I did.

All I needed to do was tell myself a new story. A true story, perhaps, actually *the* true story – the story about a woman that had lived life saying yes to the fires, a woman of strength and integrity and determination and courage – in fact, the story that everyone around me was telling about me as well, if only I could have put myself in their shoes.

I invite you to change your shoes, superwomen. Perhaps, in fact, it's time for some boots and a cape. Because we all have those stories that we tell ourselves, and sister-friends – they're just *stories*. And the beauty of a story is that you *get to be the author*. And there's always another chapter just waiting to be written.

With the help of some amazing guides, I changed that story. And in doing so I changed the ending. And here, in fact, is where you and I meet.

Have you ever read the story *Because a Little Bug Went KA-CHOO*? It's one of my personal fan faves in the constant march of children's books, and while it purports to explain chaos theory, my favorite takeaway is the fantastic causality that the story articulates – and the understanding that, often, our life purpose is found in battling the things that we hate about this world.

In the book, a little bug sneezes, which makes a leaf fall. The leaf falls on the head of a worm, which makes the worm MAD. The enraged worm vents his anger by kicking a bucket, which flies into the air and, eventually – through a series of wild events – causes a wild circus parade that is, as far as we know, still going on to this day.

This is a story of a little bug sneezing in my direction – and the kicking of the bucket that we've been doing ever since, creating, of course, our own wild circus parade. And I invite you to join me in this dance.

Because here's where we meet: you know how we've been weaving this story together? Well, that's why I'm now a multi-national CEO. Because my company is taking on world change, one leader at a time. And right now *you* are that leader. All of the parts of this book, all of the exercises in the workbook with your book club? They're all leadership skills. For me, when I was trained on these skills, it felt so much like these were all the skills I'd learned as a wife and a mom, I just didn't know how to articulate them. And so...here they are. Articulated for you. And we're taking women, just like you, and creating jobs and space for them to be paid to be the mothers and the community leaders and the *everything* that women have been since time immemorial and never been paid for. We're in the process of rebuilding the fantastic, world-changing parts of 1950s communities that we all so valued (minus all of the crazy parts that we so needed to throw out in the bathwater) – except now, instead of the women being the slaves at home giving all of that value to society, now they get to be paid by society for doing that same work.

And we invite you to join us.

Because, Superwomen, *society needs us*. It is currently falling on it's toosh. And someone, someone needs to look after it. And who better to do that than a bunch of cape-wearing, Prada-wielding, badass Superwomen? It's time. Oh, it's so *beyond* time to make this happen, ladies.

THOUGHT QUESTIONS

Chapters 15 through 19

1. What are the vocations that you have held - both paid and unpaid, in-the-box, and box-breaking? What are the different skills that you've learned from each one, and who have you been in each of those? What are the vocations that are still calling to you? Is there a vocation that you have seen threaded through your life, and are eager to explore? What's possible in that exploration of the new?

2. What does the "garden of your soul" look like now? Is it full of color and hedgehogs? Is it fertile Earth, waiting to take hold? What are the colors, the smells, the sounds and the feelings that are calling to you there? If that garden was on a platter as a choice for you, what choice would you make?

3. What are the quests that you've undertaken in your life? If there were one quest, buried deep in your soul, what would

it be? You know - the one that you've never told anyone? The secret quest buried down inside...what would it look like if a flashlight turned on it?

4. Choice and Free Will...What do you think about that? What are the challenges here? And what are your choices costing you now? What are you are tolerating - and what could be possible?

5. What are the dragons that you are hiding? What is possible if you bring them to light? Can you think of a story that expresses those dragons in hiding? Or are your dragons out there, tossing rocks themselves? What does that story look like?

6. What are the stories that others tell about you that you think are "just too much"? What would it look like if that story were yours? If your life were a movie, what is the story you would want to see?

PART 4

SPARK

Chapter 20

THE FIRES SWEEPING
ACROSS US ALL

There's something going on right now in history, something that I can't quite put my finger on. Something around walking through fires collectively, and a gift given to all of us. Can you feel it too? Does it feel like dusty wind blowing in your face, or the shaking of shoes too long covered with dirt? It's something. And it's calling to us.

Sister-friends, the twentieth century was *hard*. From the hideous trenches and mustard gas of World War I, to the agonizing screech and terrifying repetition of World War II to the atom bomb of unending silence and the horrors in the jungles and mountains and civil wars of nations, this past century burned, burned, burned. We watched as people fought and struggled out of the cocoon to win semblances of freedom, while those that led us all were shot and destroyed in the lead vanguards through the fire. It was *hard*. And it was *real*. It was some of the most authentic suffering I've ever heard of and heard from the mouths of those that lived through it. And while

I was most certainly *not* a part of it, I saw that suffering and agony in the broken marriages, broken adolescences, broken screaming that I witnessed all around me. The generations before us fought the good fight, walked through that fire with the coals burning into their souls, and I was the witness to the agonizing aftermath that attended that brokenness. And while we all walk through our own fires – or don't, as we choose – there is something calling about us walking through them together, collectively, while holding each other's hands – and the boon that comes to us all for having done so.

Chapter 21

SPARK, 1.0 – DISBELIEF

I kind of never knew what I wanted to do in life, you know? Always really good at school and with the curse of the most supportive mom ever, I fell into that middle-area malaise of being told (and believing) that I could do anything – and was completely stymied by too many choices to even begin to know where to start on doing *my* thing. This is a completely ridiculous problem when compared to the other problems in the world, I know. And yet, I reference you back to the very beginning of this book. No one gets the monopoly on pain. And whatever we struggle with in the moment is our hardest struggle. And let me tell you – for teenage me, this was a very large struggle. And feeling like a wandering nothing, bouncing from place to place as I tried to grasp onto an outpost that might give my life meaning? That was most definitely scary and painful.

And so, to fix that, I decided to run away on my own. It was a good choice.

Before heading off to university, I spent a summer living on St John (the Virgin Island), working at an eco resort. Yes, much had changed since those poor, cockroach-laden days – and I had had the gumption from somewhere to not only fill out and fax in (yep, fax) the application, but to then get onto a flight and land in an island that I barely knew, to take a ferry to an even more unknown island and cross my fingers that someone would be there to help me figure out the next step.

Aaaaaand...no one was there.

It was the greatest gift I could have been given.

So let me clarify something about this right here. It most definitely did *not* seem like a gift in the moment. In fact, it was freaking terrifying. I was dropped off by a slightly-scary taxi driver, standing in the open-air restaurant of the resort with my huge-ass bag (sooooo many shoes), with literally not one clue as to what to do next. And so, ummmm...what do you do in that situation? I kind of wandered around, and finally found some note somewhere that told me where my tent was. And so I lugged my *gigantic* bag up the boardwalk stairs (I still always pack too many shoes), dying of sweat and finally collapsing in this open-air permanent-structure tent that I was going to call my own for the next two months.

It was paradise.

This was the beginning of my solo journeys, my errands to push myself and discover more about just what I could actually do. This was the first hit in my addiction to being a wild adventuress, and was the first foot-placement on the path that led me to the Singing Gypsy Lioness that I claim today.

And...I get ahead of myself.

I spent that summer getting to know myself and my world a bit more. And let me tell you something. I *fell in love* with the world. Hopelessly, heart-stoppingly, head-over-heels in love with this world. Because, y'all, it's *beautiful*. And as I dove into those blue turtle-filled turquoise waters after my early-morning shift as the breakfast cook, as I lay on that hot sand and fell asleep and soaked up all of the sun-heat, as I played at night with the phosphorescence in the Caribbean night-waters and watched the dancing of the light on the purple sea fans, I fell more and more and more in love with this world, and saw the incredible array of amazingness that it gives to us all. I felt the healing power of forgiveness of the Earth for all of the anger and sadness and fear that we pour into it over and over. And I saw more and more the destruction that we were creating in this incredible love-nest around us.

And at the same time, as I spent the evenings in my tent smoking my cigarettes over and over and hiding from everyone – even my hot summer boyfriend and newly made friends – and writing in my journal and trying to figure out this newly emerging image of myself, I made a tacit agreement with something that was deep and living inside of me. I made the soul-destroying agreement that I wasn't really strong enough or good enough to actually do any of the things that I was being called to do. No, in fact, it was more than that. I was an asshole, an arrogant, mean, and soon-to-be friendless ass-hole if I lived life as shinily as it was calling me to be.

Recently I was talking with my daughter about how to navigate the waters of early adolescence, and I told her something that I like to say to myself a lot these days. We women? We have this thing where we think that if we shine really brightly it's going to dim the lights of all of the women around us. Like, it's going to make them all feel bad that their lights aren't shining that brightly too. And so we look around and say to ourselves "Oh, I'm not going to talk about how awesome I am. I'm not going to say all of the fantastic things I'm doing. In fact, I'm not even going to do those things, because these women? They're not going to be my friends if I do that. And they're all going to feel bad about themselves, and *I love them* and I would never want them to feel that way. So...screw that. I'm going to just dim it all down a little bit, because that will make them feel better."

Complete. Hooey.

Do you know why? Do you know what happens when we do that? Follow it to the logical conclusion, sister-friends. I know you can see where that logic breaks down.

If I'm dimming my light to make other women feel better, and they're all doing the same thing for me, then *all of our lights just get collectively smaller and smaller as we try to make each other feel better about each other.*

It's the tragedy of the commons, played out in Superland.

And do you know what else? It's a *complete* lie from the devil. You want to talk about the devil and Prada. This one is a total lie. And it's keeping us all down.

I want to tell you the other side of that story that I've started living out in the past few years. It's a story where I've said *screw you* and just started living my life shining as brightly as I know how. And do you know what that's done?

It's given permission to all of the women around me to do the same.

As I've been off flying around the world, creating my own company, raising children in my way, running marathons and wearing badass boots and not caring and not judging others, I'm all of a sudden approached constantly by all of these women saying things like "How do you do it all?" and "How are you *constantly* smiling?" and "What's your secret?" and "You are literally one of the most inspirational women that I've ever met." And I think to myself w*hat is wrong with all of us if I'm one of the most inspirational women they've ever met?* Because hell yes I have a fantastic diamond. *And so do we all.* What the crap is wrong with us that we're not all shining it like mad and taking on the world? Because, if I learned one thing in St John, it's that the world needs us desperately.

And so ...yeah. My first story of my spark is one of disbelief. Because for so long – for *so long* I didn't think that I was really all that special. And while I would do some of the things, it was like a secret society where I didn't show any other women that I was doing that because maybe that would make them feel bad. And then I might be rejected from society. And that would make me the Other. And...in our primitive cave-woman brains, being the other means death. And so, for so long, I dimmed my light in order to try to convince everyone of how much I was just like them. The irony, of course, was when I found out that we all, in fact, are the Other. We just don't know it yet.

Chapter 22

THE OTHER

Being in the Army branch of the military, we spent our first years stationed in the most middle-of-absolutely nowhere postings humanly possible. Our first middle-of-nowhere was in Ft. Benning, Georgia. And it was freaking amazing.

You know when you have to do something and have really, really low expectations, and it ends up being completely incredible? That was us and Georgia (deep south 'murica Georgia, not the right-by-Ukraine-and-Armenia Georgia). Being an environmentalist obsessed with nature, I fell in love with the wild beauty of the area, and felt my heart tearing as I learned that the lush green kudzu vine that I thought was so beautiful was actually invasive and destroying the area. I died a thousand deaths when we drove into this tiny southern town, and I fell in love with the slowness and community-ness of the South.

It was not without its confusions of course – for no story is uncomplicated.

We moved from Georgia to North Carolina, staying in the South and inculcating ourselves into this new world. And while it was beautiful, it didn't come without its problems. First, I couldn't get a job in my chosen field – at least not immediately. Being an environmental economist, I found quite scant interest in such a leftie way of thinking there in those bright red states. And having chosen to be a slave of my husband's career, I had little option but to make do with what became available.

The second huge stumbling block that I encountered was the racism that was seeped into what seemed the fabric of existence there. My husband and I remarked, as we drove cross country in our moving van, that the people just got nicer and nicer as we moved farther and farther South. And while we may have not been able to understand them – try setting up your utilities over the phone with someone from the Deep South when you've only just arrived – we felt their warmth and caring and compassion much more than anything we ever felt in Seattle. And we *loved* it. It is beautiful and gracious and really, in my opinion, the way we should be with each other.

And we quickly learned that it was only because we were white.

I remember one time in particular walking through the Piggly Wiggly (yes, people. It is actually a place) and realizing that I felt some weird barrier between myself and all of the non-white people. Having grown up in mostly whitey-Ville (hello, Nebraska in the 80s and 90s), I had just never felt that...energetic wall before. Having read the stories and history of the Deep South, I understand it more now. And it still breaks my heart.

As I am an insanely optimistic person, I feel like I try so hard to hold true to my values of radical inclusion and radical love – and try to manifest them in this world. And I tried to do that, at least a bit, while living in the South. And the battle came to roost in my soul from a casual (yes, obscenely casual) comment from one of my neighbors – "I'm fine with my daughter going out with one of them blacks, but one of those Mexicans? No way."

Hurl my breath into a vacuum of despair. Not one thing about that statement was ok.

And so, as I fell in love with the South and the gentle welcoming breezes of conversation and neighborliness that held me in that cocoon, I also felt the shattering of my beautiful rose-colored glasses, and the need to make newer, stronger, and wiser frames. Because *yes,* the South is beautiful and gracious and lovely. And *yes*, the South is still stuck with massive racism and other-ing. And because no story is uncomplicated, I want to say something specific right here. This is a box. This is a total generalization of the South. I have put the people of the South into a box with this story. And while I didn't get that then, I do get it now – after the second half of this story, where we, instead, were the other.

After living in the South for almost 5 years – and truly loving it while we were there – we found ourselves on the plane to what seemed the opposite – to the lush, wave-soaked islands of Hawaii.

Ohhhh, Hawaii. Hawaii is where we lost ourselves, found insanely phenomenal friends, discovered our own strengths, and basically really grew up. Hawaii is also where we found ourselves put into a box, over and over – and started living the life of the other that we've continued living to this day.

I remember one day in particular, when our 16-year-old babysitter told us that she "knew what we mainlanders were like, because she watched *The Hills*." As in, we were all Heidi and Spencer, with massive amounts of money and anything we wanted – while they were stuck dealing with massive land prices, teenage pregnancy, and meth problems.

Take my breath away, once again.

Soooo...here's the rub. In the South, I wasn't the Other – because I was white. However, I "othered" everyone there in making these generalizations about Southerners. When I moved to Hawaii, all of a sudden I found myself in the minority, and myself as the Other. And I realized what it was like to have those generalizations made about me.

Having grown up in a most decidedly *not*-Hills life, I decided then and there that it was a part of my job to break these boxes that were being put around me and all other mainlanders. And, in turn, to allow my own boxes to be broken about others.

I tell my kiddos these days that we all have boxes – and that's ok. Boxes help us to organize the world. They're kind of like the stories we tell ourselves in our heads about what's going on around us all of the time. And if we didn't have those boxes – if we had no stereotypes or archetypes or whatever you want to call them – we couldn't even get out of bed in the morning. Because we'd be looking at the floor going "is that floor really a floor? I mean, is it really solid? Because I know that some of those atoms could be on the other side of the Universe, so perhaps if I step down and put my foot there there will be nothing" and we would just spend the whole day doing *that*. Boxes help us to organize life and focus on the things that we really want to focus on. So if, for example, we actually are quantum physicists, we can ponder all day on the floor and where the atoms are. For the rest of us, we put that floor into our "solid objects are solid" box and move on to what we need to accomplish.

And it's like we do that with everything. We need those boxes to just get *on* with life. And our boxes are all up on a shelf, just waiting for us. And occasionally we need to reach up and pluck down one of the boxes, unpack it and look at it in a different way. And maybe we need to break that box, see what it looks like as a new creation...and then, perhaps, put it back up on that shelf to live in that new form until another breaking is needed.

That's what I like to think about the boxes we carry around about the world around us.

What I've come to realize is that, in fact, *none* of us are inside a box. I mean – everyone puts us into boxes. I'm put in the box of military wife, of stay-at-home-mom, of CEO, of entrepreneur, of marathoner, of woman, of midwesterner, of American...I mean, you name it. I've got lots of boxes. And while those boxes are true, not one of those boxes is *me*. Which means, frankly, freedom. Because if none of those boxes is me...that means I live in the in-between. And the in-between is where boxes are broken – if only we have the courage to break them.

Chapter 23

SPARK 2.0 – APATHY

On the day of our marriage – really, the time period when I entered into the adult world – I was a jumble of *all of the things*. And while I was so, so happy to be marrying this man that I loved desperately, I was also terribly, terribly sad to be leaving behind single Carmen. Because I *loved* single Carmen. She was so fun and feisty and free-spirited and strong strong strong, strong to the depths of the earth, like a baobab tree with roots below Africa. She was wild and independent and un-tamed, and she had served me so well as I was growing through life on my own. I loved her so. And I knew I was going to miss her. And not only that, but I was collapsing two things together – I was telling myself this story that, in marrying this military man, I was giving up my personal dreams, dreams to join the Peace Corps (I told you, hippie), of moving to New York City and living the *Sex and the City* life, of entering politics and government and changing the world and saving the planet. And I told myself this story that, because I was marrying him and following him to the environmental backwaters of the world (hello, Georgia), I was also giving up on my dream and putting on long-term hold the life I dreamed of leading. I saw it as an either/or sort of question, and I chose him over me.

Oh, the stories we tell ourselves. Thank goodness life gives us so many chances to unravel our own convoluted logic.

I remember one afternoon, about four years after the birth of our first child and two years after the arrival of our second, lying on the floor of our tiny box of a condo in Hawaii, just waiting silently as the children napped. And I remember the Earth calling out to me (weird, I know, and it *happened*), and feeling the groan deep within this Mother Earth that we'd been given – a groan and a weeping that could only be heard in the abject silence in which I waited. And I remember feeling my heart tear in two, because while I knew this was happening, I felt helpless to do anything about it – for I had chosen a different path.

I had chosen the vocation of wifedom and parenthood instead of political activism, and it seemed there was no space for *me*, my life purpose, my spark, within that arena.

And I wept.

I remember lying on that floor, feeling the cheap carpet on my back, hearing the earth-cries from the deep underneath, and living the agony of believing that I couldn't do anything about it and *saying no to the call*. And do you know what that feels like?

I'm thinking that it's possible that maybe you do. I'm not sure, and I'm just wondering if maybe you've felt that feeling too. If maybe, maybe I'm not alone in this. I don't know – and I'm so curious to know who else has been there.

I've always loved that story in the Odyssey, when Ulysses passes by the bay of the sirens. Do you remember this part? It's the part where he ties himself to the mast, and implores his sailing crew to ignore everything he says and plugs up their ears with cotton, because he wants to hear the beautiful, the enchanting, the voluptuous singing of the sirens – and not get pulled into their snare. And as he's listening to this song, and revelling with delight, he starts weeping and gnashing his teeth and imploring his men to stop the vessel and turn in to shore, for to ignore those songs meant death.

Oh, that siren song is powerful.

There was a woman that lived on the street where I grew up that I admired immensely. I used to babysit for the family, and I adored and felt so drawn to her passion and energy. She was so alive, so *full*, so brimming over with her-ness, all within this small midwestern city, on a normal suburban street.

I heard a few years after I went to college that she had left her family, divorcing her husband and fleeing to Africa to do missionary work.

She had heard the call of the sirens, and she had answered their rapturous song.

And as I laid there on the carpet in that broken Hawaiian paradise, I believed that that was the only option available to me. I heard that same call, and I lay weeping and writhing because I hadn't uncovered the truth.

I was still tied to the masthead. And, like Ulysses, it almost drove me mad.

It would be many, many years until I learned that the struggle through the masthead had actually granted me an immense, irreplaceable gift. And that my apathy in that moment – my rejection of the call – had taught me just how terrible it is to say no when the Universe calls your name.

Chapter 24

FREE WILL IS A B

In life, there come a few pivotal moments of destiny. Those moments when the Universe reaches out, offers a hand, and asks "are you ready?" These moments can be terrifying, of course. In fact, in my experience, terror and uncertainty are the absolute certainties that populate these moments. In looking back on these moments in my life, I am always reminded of *Indiana Jones and the Last Crusade*. Remember when Indiana steps out into the unknown? After having gone through all the trials – to include snakes, falls into the abyss, tests of cognition and memory and humility (not to mention whirling blades and arrows), finally, finally Indie gets to that last point, the last moment before reaching what his heart is calling out to him – and finds himself confronted with a valley of indecision in front of him. Being the movies, this is of course a literal as well as figurative valley, with no bridge and sheer cliffs, which he has to cross in order to reach the holy grail. And here he has a choice – and it is, of course, *his* choice, with no judgement or misperceptions – to turn around, and diminish, and stay as he is, or to take that leap of faith into the abyss, and maybe, maybe, maybe claim that shiny star that is waiting for his future.

Have you ever been at that point of decision? I have. Many times. Usually I didn't actually *feel* it was a point of decision until much later. At the time I just felt that something was tugging at my heart, and I also knew that there was no way of doing it and it was beyond terrifying. Oh, my constant refrain of "I know, yes I know" has been my battle – because that ever-knowing only lives in our heads, and our faith lives in a much deeper part of our truths, doesn't it?

Because, in the end, I think that maybe that's a big part of the puzzle. Faith in ourselves – that yes, we really are as incredible and strong and amazing as we think we are on the inside. Faith in our world – yes, it really *is* as beautiful as we envision it to be, and people really are that spectacular. And faith in the Universe – faith that, if I take that first step out, there will be something there to help me, I won't have to do it alone, that somehow, somehow, it will all work out okay, even if my logical, amazing, great big brain can't figure out how that will be. Because sometimes things are just mystical and illogical, until afterwards when we can logic it away. Faith that it will, really, all turn out as my heart is telling me it will turn out, because the world *so* needs this, and I don't know how to make it happen, I just know that the Universe is calling my heart to take that first step.

And here's the rub about that first step. Do you remember that part in the movie? Indie had *no* idea how it was going to work out. None. Not one. In fact, he pretty much believed (or at least this is what I got from the look on his face) that he was going to fall. And I mean – fall into the abyss and *die*. Frankly, I get that feeling too. I've been on that ledge multiple times, and so often I've felt I just couldn't do it because I'd be mocked (to death, as it feels) or look like an idiot or fail in front of others and be ostracized or just die because it hurt too much on the inside or prove to myself just how much of a failure I fear I might be. And to me, on that ledge, those feelings are so strong, and so terrifying, that it felt like a literal death was a possibility – and every part of my being shrank away from that cliff face. There have been many a time, in fact, when I've turned around and walked away. And, oh, looking back on those moments – those are the only moments in my life that I regret. Sadly, that knowing hasn't made jumping off future cliffs any easier. Yep. Uber. Bummer. What it *has* done is made me have much more faith in myself, have a bit more belief that I really am as amazing as I think I might be on the inside – and that faith, of course, has made me a Superwoman. Because all Superwoman needs is the belief that she can fly, not the knowledge of how to do it. Frankly, my current cliff-diving strategy is to hit them at a dead run and jump with my eyes closed. Still haven't mastered the art of looking as I'm leaping.

There is another story here that keeps nagging and tugging at my heart, and so I think maybe it needs to be said here.

I have often, in my life, come to those points of decision – those choices that the Universe holds out in front of me – and felt like I *couldn't* make the decision because of something – or someone – else that was populating my life at that point. I couldn't get that job, because we were just about to move away. I couldn't volunteer or help out, because I had small kid-dos at home and I needed to tend to them. And when, later on, I was faced with a marriage that didn't fit with my values, I couldn't stay with him because he had betrayed me so much. They – the amorphous they – had taken away my choice, my freedom to choose, because of the decisions they had made, or the position in which they had put me.

To which I say **NEVERMORE**.

The amorphous "they" having the power to take away my choices? That, my friend, is a lie. It's pretty much the biggest lie that is out there. Do you know why? Because no one – *no one* – can take away your freedom to choose. Yep. For reals. No one.

Do you know why I decided to stay with my husband after he betrayed me? Why I decided to fly to Africa that first time, having *no idea* what I was going to do there or who I was going to meet? Why I chose to start my own business and fail and fail and fail and look ridiculous to the world for *years* and keep plugging at it even as I cried at my desk every day? Do you know why? Because when I am 90 years old and have to look at myself in the mirror, who do I have to answer to? Is it my husband? Society? My friends? My children? My DOG? Nope. Abso-freakin-lutely not. When I am 90 years old I've got *no one else* to answer to but myself. And when I look at myself and say "So, sister-friend, how did *that* go? How did it play out, that life, that one chance in a trillion to live here on Earth? How did we do with that?" I am going to have to look myself in the eyeball and respond. And let me tell you, it is not going to fly if that response is "well, I *really* wanted to change the world in this one way, but I couldn't because I had kids and I didn't know what to do" or "because I was scared" or "because these people were mean to me" or "because he betrayed me" or "because I had hard things happen to me in my childhood." Have you hung out with many 90 year olds recently? Let me tell you something – that kind of logic does *not* fly with them. 90 years olds don't listen to those lies – all of the prevarications and justifications fall away when we're old, and we let our boobs flop all over the place and say *all the things* because 90 year-olds just don't freaking care anymore – those lies don't work on them anymore and they can acknowledge out loud the truth. It's not that they're crazy – it's just that they've let go of the social veneer we all hold to be "appropriate" and they say all of the things that everyone else is harboring deep in their souls.

And so goes you, sister-friend, when you are 90 years old.

Think about it. Look your 90 year old self in the mirror, and try some of those excuses on her. Does she raise her eyebrow? Cackle in your face? Shake her finger and shake her head and put her hand on her hip and start calling you a liar?

So guess what? This is your future. And, more than that – it is inevitable. One day you will be that person, looking back at yourself in the mirror. What do you want to be saying? Do you want to be berating yourself, frustrated and angry and hungering for death because you just "never got the chance" to do all of the things that you really wanted to be doing? Or do you want to be fist-bumping and drinking margaritas and saying "come get me, next 50 years of life, I'm ready to make more amaze-balls happen" and cackling about all of the crazy and wild and fantastic things you did in life that completely fell apart and also magically, somehow, worked out in the end?

Do you know why I stayed with my husband, why I work and live in dangerous areas with the most vulnerable people, why I keep working *hard* to raise my kids, why I keep getting up off my ass from my well-deserved rest and *keep doing life*? Because no matter what – *no matter what* – no one can take my choice to LIVE away from me. No one can take my choice to answer my call, to be that person that I know I really am, deep down inside, away from me. When I was young and dreamed of my future and said I was going to be married forever and go out and fix the world and raise amazing children, *I freaking meant it.* That's *my* code of honor. And it doesn't matter what my husband or my children or the world or anyone ever does – they can spit on me, my husband can divorce me, my children can turn out to be drug dealers and prostitutes – it doesn't matter, because I can still live out *my* dreams, can't I? I can still remain married to my husband in my heart, to the end of my days. I can still work every single day to love on and support and give discipline and wisdom to my children, no matter what their choices are. I can keep going out and making a difference in the world as I see fit, no matter if anyone else decides to come with. That's *my* choice. And no one – not my husband, my children, the world – nor anyone else, can ever take that away from me.

That's the blessing and the curse of free will, sister-friends. The blessing is that no one, *no one* can ever take that choice away from you. The curse is that you have to leap into the terrifying unknown and just hang on for dear life that it will all turn out alright. It's good the Universe has a sense of humor, isn't it?

Chapter 25

SPARK 3.0 –
PLAYING CAT AND MOUSE

"What did I give them?"

I have struggled and wrestled and fought with that question – posed to me many moons ago by a wonderful mentor and friend – and I still haven't come up with a satisfactory answer. Hope? Space? The Permission to Dream? I haven't been able to find the answer, and I've finally moved to a place where I feel like it's not the answer, but the question itself that needs resolving. For, indeed, it feels to me that it hasn't been a one-way street – that, in fact, these women – through their strength, tenacity, and openness – have given me so much more in the creation together. In fact, it feels like the question should, instead, be "what did we create together?" And the answer to that, of course is simple. We created wings.

A while ago I travelled to Kenya for the first time, in pursuit of a Spark that had been calling my name. This was a trip I had long been called to take, and always found reasons why it wouldn't work – not enough money, we had small children at home that I needed to take care of, we were most likely moving to Africa in the future so why would I go now? I found all of the excuses to massage my frightened soul, intent upon covering up that diamond because it seemed the glare of the sparkles was just too much. I deflected the ever-present tug on my heart until I was asked to be coached on a "radical action" in front of a workshop of peers. I said yes, only because I "wanted to help others learn" – and I found instead the permission to fly. An amazing man – and wonderful coach – took all of my fears and doubts and turned them around into a kaleidoscope of colors until I, too, could see my life through that different lens. Instead of seeing my family as a barrier that was holding me back, he held them up to me as an amazing support structure that gave me a springboard for my dreams. Instead of not having the money, he shifted it to be a space for abundance and opportunity. And these few little tweaks, these few little turns of the kaleidoscope, this small step to the side and invitation to see my life from that angle, opened up the floodgates that had been locked inside my brain – and changed the course of my life forever.

Two months later I was on a plane to Kenya. I remember sitting on the plane, thinking "*What* am I doing?" I had vague plans of who I would meet, what I would discuss, and was in the process of setting up a leadership workshop with some local women in vulnerable communities. And all throughout the flight, all of those negative pirate-y voices pounded in my head, saying that I was a fool to be doing this, and nothing would come from it. And oh, they were so, so wrong.

Four days into my trip I met with a group of vulnerable women (read: extremely, extremely poor) to give them a leadership workshop. Sitting in a hut with dirt floors and no electricity, I looked around the musty filtered semi-darkness and got to know a little bit of these women around me. These women had lived lives that seemed too hard to bear – impoverished, without support, many had given up their children or grandchildren to people that promised to feed and educate the small ones – something the grinding poverty of these women's day-to-day could not afford. They had given up their babies in all good faith, believing that it was the only way for them to see a better tomorrow – only to learn, later, that they had been swindled and lied to. You see, these "orphanages" were actually institutions of human trafficking, using the children as lures to bring in well-meaning, loving tourists that paid large sums to help people in need – specifically orphans in Kenya. They used these children to entice the money into the institution, and when the voluntours (as they're called) weren't present, put the children to labor denying them even the education their mothers had been promised. The mothers and grandmothers discovered they'd been duped, but were unable to retrieve their children as no legal structures were in place to allow them to do so. Enter Stahili Foundation, a phenomenal, small, scrappy NGO that works with a bare-bones team to identify the families, use their legal and technical expertise to shut down the institutions, and repatriate the children with their families, or "The Guardians."

I was sitting in a hut surrounded by The Guardians.

We spent a short three hours together. In that time, we heard a bit of each other's stories – they heard about the loss of my daughter, I heard about how they had watched as one of their schoolmates was killed by stampeding buffalo as they walked to school one day. And we did some dreaming together, looking into the future, opening up to the possibilities of what was there, if they only walked that way. In fact, I did exactly the same thing that I do with women all over the world. And you know what?

They were exactly the same as every group of women I've ever worked with.

I've worked with International Aid organizations, governments, and friends from all over the world. And there's this thing that happened to me for a really long time. This thing where I got convicted to *do* something, to believe that I could make a difference and feel like I really needed to do it, whenever I heard about the terrible things that were going on in the news. Like, the sensational things. The ebola crisis. The refugee situation. The human trafficking in orphanages. The gangs and trauma of the Baltimore riots. The meth and domestic violence of Hawaii. And do you know what?

We are all exactly the same. We are all searching for the same answers. And, if we shared with each other – instead of being frightened, or "othered," or scared of our own brilliance because maybe that will make others feel small – if we just got over this all and started sharing our poop and our joys, our triumphs and our falls with each other? The world would be freaking brilliant, ladies.

And so, that's what my spark is doing now. It's breaking those barriers, creating the opportunities for women to get *down* with each other and really actually solve the crap that's going on around the world. Because the men have had a long enough time of trying to make it work. And now it's time for the women.

Chapter 26

UNBEARABLE STRENGTH

What if we've been playing all these years with one hand tied behind our backs?

Remember how I told you that I converted to Catholicism? Especially given my own past abuse, it's been – needless to say – pretty complicated these past few years. And as I've come to terms more and more with the abuse I myself held inside, I've taken a look at this church that I now love with all of my soul, that has helped me to recover my own brilliance, and do you know what I think?

I don't blame the abused for hating and blaming the Church. In fact, of all the people that bring me emotions about my past abuse, the ones that brought me the most loathing and anger and disgust were not the actual abuser, but the ones that stood aside and watched and did nothing.

There is an amazing quote from *Boondock Saints* that has rung true in my soul ever since I heard it. After telling a story of their own, these brothers that are walking a pent-up explosion of messianic deliverance, say "They all just watched as Kitty was being stabbed to death in broad daylight. They watched as her assailant walked away. Now, we must all fear evil men. But there is another kind of evil which we must fear most, and that is the indifference of good men."

Let me amend that a bit. Because while yes that's true...what I'm more interested in is the indifference of good women. The fear and helplessness and disbelief that we women feel in the face of the hurts of the world. The women – and I am one of them – that know about the UN Peacekeeper Babies and the raping of the earth by our insatiable consumption and the incredible, massive, terrifying disparity of wealth between the "haves" and the "have-nots" – the women, *like me*, that sit with friends and talk about safe, not-scary issues and pretend like the real, the soul-destroying, the terrifyingly agonizingly hard-ass problems of the world that we don't know how to solve are not actually happening. The women that aren't willing to look at themselves, at their own homes, at their own families and their own children and their own communities and say "something needs to be fixed here – and it's up to me to do it." The women – *and yes, ladies, I am in this space* – that are terrified *that maybe it's all my fault* – instead of empowered that *hell yes it's all my fault, which means I can absolutely do something about it* – if only I ask for help.

These are the people that sit by and do nothing. This is the kind of evil that we must fear the most. And I am totally one of them.

... What if we've been playing all these years with one hand tied behind our backs?

The people that knew about my abuse and allowed it to happen? The church that shunted priest from place to place and never brought it to light? The people that flinch and turn the TV or the radio to something less disturbing? I know what they're thinking.

Because I am one of them.

I personally have this thing of "they-ing" the problems in society. This thing where I say "well, I can't do anything about it, but *they* will." Yes. They. The big, amorphous, brother-in-the-sky they that I keep saying will take care of it all. Or the government that I keep saying "But they *should* be taking care of it." Perhaps that's true. Hell yes. And they're not. So *what now.* And do you know what is on repeat in my own head, over and over, when I see these problems?

What can I – I mean, me, just little old me – actually do to help?

There's just one of me. I don't have the skills needed to make a difference. It's too big of a problem for just one person. I might be ostracized from the group if I speak up. I don't have enough time/energy/willpower to do that. Someone else can take care of it, but no. Not me.

I spent years – *years* – when my children were small, hearing the earth cry out to me as I watched the beautiful island of Hawaii be desecrated over and over by the environmental disasters, the cover-ups for the sake of tourism, the toxic sludge and human destruction of the coral and oceans. I remember laying on the floor of our tiny tiny space and *feeling* the Aina crying out to me, and me telling back the story "what can I do? I am just one person. I am only here for a short time – nothing I do will make a lasting impact. Not only that, but when I try to do something, I fall down and fail and it doesn't actually work. No one will listen to me. I have small children, I really can't do anything because I need to look after them and no one will let me help when I have kids in tow. I'm sorry I'm sorry I'm sorry and I am not powerful enough to do anything about it."

And do you know what that story said back to me?

It killed my soul.

That brilliance, that wonder, that amazingness within me that had withstood decades of abuse and fire-walking and pain – that light was finally infected by the darkness when I started telling myself that they were too big and I was too small. And I started believing the lie that my power wasn't strong enough.

... What if we've been playing all of these years with one hand tied behind our backs?

Can I tell you something? Nothing, nothing, nothing that those people of my youthful indifference say or do would ever make it better. Nothing. Not a damn thing. And I can forgive my abuser more readily that I can forgive those that stood by. Deep in my bones, for sure and absolutely, the only thing I can ever do to rise from the ashes is to take ahold of my own power. To *love* it fiercely, all of it – the joys and the triumphs and the falls and the vulnerability – and to stand up again and say "this is my fight to fight."

And here it's time for me to turn my green lioness cat eyes on you and say

"I see you. I see your hurts. I see your agonies. I see your story, my friend. And it is *your* story, whole and breathless and painful painful painful and powerful and real. It is a story of a heroine that has been beaten, been put down, been hurt by the world and has stood up over and over and over again and Kept.Moving.Forward."

What if we've been playing all this time with one hand tied behind our back?

Can I ask you a question? What if it is time for all of us superwomen to rise from the ashes? What if it is time to embrace our weakness and see the truth of our power? Good God, what if all this time, we haven't known that the fall is what made us unbearably strong? What if it is time to turn to the evil that is telling us we're not good enough, we're not skilled enough, we're only here because they put us here and say to them:

Perhaps, all these years we've been playing with one hand tied behind our backs.

What if it is our weaknesses that are our greatest superpowers? What if it is our self-doubt and unconfidence and fear of being found out as a fraud that, in fact, makes us unstoppable? What if, of all the stories we tell about ourselves, it is the ones where we tried and failed that make us whole? What if our power is our ability to absorb all of the pain and agony and brokenness of the world over and over and over, and stand up time after time with glorious grace and love? What if, in our trying and falling, we are giving fuel to the greatest source of power the world has ever known? What if all we have to do is run toward the scariest places as hard as we can without trying to prove anything to anyone and with tthe knowledge that we are here, not to fight the battle, but to end it – and to fall, over and over again? What if we could run into danger, saying – you may not have come here to fight this fight, but I DID – *knowing* that we will fall, and realizing that ***in the fall we create unbearable strength***? What if, all this time, we've been powerful beyond measure?

One of my favorite quotes from Carol Danvers (aka Captain Marvel) is "Have you ever seen a little girl run so fast she falls down? There's an instant, a fraction of a second, before the world catches hold of her again...A moment when she's outrun every doubt and fear she's ever had about herself – and she flies.

At that moment, every little girl flies."

Time to fly, Superwomen.

Lord, grant me the glory to live in sunshine,
The promise to give me courage
The strength to carry on
And the grace to do it beautifully

THOUGHT QUESTIONS

Chapters 20 through 26

1. Do you have a "first story" of your Spark? If it were an adventure to a new place, what would that story be? Where would it be? Would it be filled with confusion and doubt, or certainty? And what would you be doing and discovering in that story?

2. For the author, the common themes of love for nature and passion for women run through all of her Spark stories. If there was a common thread in your Spark stories, something (or somethings) that have colored the weave a specific dye over and over, what would they be for you?

3. Where have you been the Other? What feelings have been present there? How are you the Other now? What are all of the angels that are possible in that situation?

4. What are the boxes that you place around yourself? That others place around you? What does your intuition tell you about this? What's the urge here?

5. Do you have a story of "laying on the floor and feeling helpless" while the world called to you to do something? Think back...any time when you were angry angry angry or sad to tears about something that was going on...and you said no? I don't know if you have been, and I'm so curious to know if I'm not alone in this? What did it feel like to you?

6. Had any good leaps of faith in your life? Looking back on them, what can you say about them now? How did it feel right before the leap? During the leap? After the leap? What's under there?

7. What are the hard, the terrifying, the strangling problems of the world that you want to talk about with your friends? If it were ok, what would you say about it? What's available for you after saying it? What's possible now?

START YOUR OWN CLUB*

Becoming Superwoman

FIERCELY YOURSELF?
COURAGEOUSLY DOING?
RADICALLY INCLUSIVE?

CLAIM FULL COPYRIGHT ON YOUR FUTURE.

BUILD REAL FRIENDSHIPS	LEADERSHIP TRAINING	FACILITATOR INCOME
Join with friends for a six-part book club meetup. Read the book, explore your own inner superwoman, & grow the friendships you've always known were possible.	Every month, meet online with facilitators worldwide & get Aina's world-renown leadership training. Learn how to lead your book clubs & find the fantastic in everyone.	Not only will you learn your own Superwoman life & share it with friends, you'll get paid, too - because the value of Superwomen to our communities is desperately needed.
FREE	**FREE**	**BETTER THAN FREE**

*Go to ainagiving.com/becomingsuperwoman/ to start your club today.

ABOUT THE AUTHOR

Carmen Westbrook is a one-time stay-at-home-mom turned multinational CEO and entrepreneur. A mom of three, dedicated wife, and fluffy dog owner, Carmen has lived and worked as a world-class leadership development professional on four continents and five countries around the globe. Bringing humor, depth of experience, joy, and courage into the ordinary for leaders worldwide, Carmen grows leadership in organizations, communities, and vulnerable populations in the pursuit of a community-sustained future. Having conducted countless *Becoming Superwoman* workshops worldwide in addition to her company's bespoke corporate programs, Westbrook has personally seen the transformation possible in women that grow their personal leadership in safe havens of friend- and community-based clubs. Carmen lives with her family in their current hometown in Italy and travels the world as often as possible to spend time with her forever-crew of phenomenal sister-friends.